BE A
PLANT-BASED
WOMAN
WARRIOR

AVERY
an imprint of Penguin Random House
New York

BE A
PLANT-BASED
WOMAN WARRIOR

Live Fierce, Stay Bold, Eat Delicious

◄► ◄► ◄► ◄► ◄► ◄► ◄►

Jane Esselstyn
and Ann Crile Esselstyn

AVERY

an imprint of Penguin Random House LLC
penguinrandomhouse.com

Photographs by Karin McKenna

Most Avery books are available at special quantity
discounts for bulk purchase for sales promotions,
premiums, fund-raising, and educational needs.
Special books or book excerpts also can be
created to fit specific needs. For details, write
SpecialMarkets@penguinrandomhouse.com.

ISBN 9780593328910
Ebook ISBN 9780593328927

Printed in China
ScoutAutomatedPrintCode

Book design by Ashley Tucker

The recipes contained in this book have been
created for the ingredients and techniques
indicated. The Publisher is not responsible for your
specific health or allergy needs that may require
supervision. Nor is the Publisher responsible for
any adverse reactions you may have to the recipes
contained in the book, whether you follow them as
written or modify them to suit your personal
dietary needs or tastes.

To Caldwell B. Esselstyn Jr., MD, Essy, Daddy—whose steady hand and persistence in the plant-based arena have helped forge the path for strong, fierce Plant-Based Women Warriors toward a delicious future.

And to every Plant-Based Woman Warrior out there swinging from limb to limb. Keep moving forward; the best is yet to come.

CONTENTS

Introduction: Hear Us Roar 11

CHAPTER 1
How Plants Powerfully
Support Women 21

CHAPTER 2
Create Delicious 39

CHAPTER 3
The Plant-Based
Woman Warrior Kitchen 45

CHAPTER 4
Powerful Breakfasts 53

CHAPTER 5
Secret Weapons:
Sauces, Hummus,
Dressings, Salsas,
and a Guacamole 75

CHAPTER 6
Sandwich-Craft
and Beautiful Soups 109

CHAPTER 7
Warrior Salads 145

CHAPTER 8
Tofu and Tempeh,
Tasty Additions 165

CHAPTER 9
Appetizers, Sides,
and Clever Extras 177

CHAPTER 10
Crackers, Quick Breads,
and Other Fillers 201

CHAPTER 11
Build Your Own Bowls,
Handheld Meals,
and Dinner Feasts 215

CHAPTER 12
Dreamy, Daring, and
Delicious Desserts 273

Acknowledgments 312

Index 315

INTRODUCTION:
HEAR US ROAR

◁▷ ◁▷ ◁▷ ◁▷ ◁▷ ◁▷ ◁▷

We are Plant-Based Women Warriors and this is our front line.

A call to arms for vitality and uncompromised health.

A rallying cry for booming energy and rejection of disease.

Join us as we press onward with plants, love, and each other.

Be a Plant-Based Woman Warrior.

Live fierce.

Stay bold.

Eat delicious.

The fiercest person I know is my mother, Ann—and how lucky that we live next door to each other. Ann's energy and "hop-to" are my daily dose of "hell yeah." Try to keep up with her at eighty-six years old—it is exhausting! In a single day, it is not unusual to see her run, lift weights, sweep, rake, do yoga, haul brush, plant gardens, cook, and shop. She does not stop: Activity and engagement are Ann's perpetual states.

We attend a Wednesday yoga class together, and even though she prefers to be in the back row, she still catches everyone's eye. There she is, balanced in half-moon on one leg, holding a side plank without shaking, and flipping her downward dog like a gymnast. People always ask me after class, "How old is your mom?!" and hastily add, "I want to be her when I grow up!" Ha, I do, too! She has completely redefined aging and stayed in the game. Sometimes, I'm asked if my mom and I are twins. What a compliment! I can only hope to have Ann's energy and spunk as I grow older.

While trail running, Ann once impaled her lower leg on a branch. Around this time, she had been reading a book about Genghis Khan's unruly, violent upbringing, and so she figured she could handle a branch piercing her calf. She arrived at home looking fresh from a battle on the Mongolian steppes, with blood streaming down her leg. The ensuing IV antibiotics and gaping wound had her bedbound for a day. Point being, it takes a lot to momentarily impede this Plant-Based Woman Warrior.

What is the secret to Ann's way of life? What stokes her furnace every day? The answer is simple—a plant-based diet. And daily, she feasts on more food than most other humans!

My parents say they eat a plant-based diet because they want to live long and die fast. My father, Dr. Caldwell Esselstyn Jr., has been researching the link between a plant-based diet and heart disease for decades. His intense interest was our family's initiation to this way of eating. At first, Ann learned to create healthy, simple, plant-based recipes for my father's heart patients. But soon, her motivation became stronger when patients reported other lifestyle-related diseases falling away. Along with plummeting cholesterol and normalizing blood pressure, eating plant-based leveled their blood sugar, reversed erectile dysfunction and autoimmune disease symptoms, and sent their energy levels skyrocketing.

We should all accept the challenge to live long and die fast! The effect would be staggering: less medication, disease, and long-term care, and more living, activity, and—flat out—more quality time with those you love. You may be thinking, How can the answer to the many faces of lifestyle-related diseases and suffering be plants? It seems too simple. But we have seen the power of this way of eating too many times not to share and shout this message over the garden wall and from the mountaintops. There can truly be boundless health and hope ahead with a whole food, plant-based diet.

Ann is fierce! When it comes to plant-based eating, we are three generations strong, due to Ann's love and delicious persistence. She has charmed every single one in our family of twenty to be plant-based. She is a role model for giving things a go. She'll challenge grandchildren to eat their sweet potato skins, she'll harvest tall unknown weeds from the garden when out of greens, or she'll serve up "witches' brew" (as the grandchildren call it) for breakfast (see Ann's Warrior Oats, page 59) on Christmas morning. Ann is completely unapologetic about sticking with this way of eating. As my husband, Brian, says, "Ann is a bully for good." Always ready to roar at anyone about eating plants.

Here is how Ann's ten grandchildren feel about being plant-based:

GEORGIE, age eight.
Without being plant-based, I can't imagine how I'd live. I'd open the refrigerator and see things like chicken wrapped in plastic and just feel like, "WHAT HAPPENED?"

ZEB, age twenty.
It checks every box: not killing anything, great for the planet, not burdened by being sick, you feel good. It's the future.

GUS, age twenty-five.
Plant-based makes me feel forever strong, forever capable, forever grounded, and excited about a healthy tomorrow.

HOPE, age seven.
If you eat meat, you die.

CRILE, age twenty-two.
Plant-based is empowering for me, revolutionary for the world, creative, and always a talking point with my friends and coaches. I feel empowered when I can educate them about it and be a living, breathing example of it.

SOPHIE, age eleven.
Whenever I eat good food, I feel good, and whenever I eat unhealthy food, something in my stomach just feels wrong. I'm lucky because it's been easy for me since I've been plant-strong my whole life. Being plant-based doesn't mean just eating salads all the time; it means so many fun, unique things like a kale cake with raspberry frosting. Not just vanilla frosting with pink dye in it, but lemons and raspberries and it's just really fun and tasty!

FLINN, age twenty-seven.
Plant-based is the definition of our family. It has brought us together to be creative and show our skills in different areas; it's our thing and the one common thing we all branch off from and that makes us connect.

ROSE, age twenty-two.
Plant-based makes me feel free and has saved me from the emotionally turbulent diet of restriction so many friends in their twenties are caught in.

BAINON, age nineteen.
Right now, I love being plant-based because I know what I'm putting in my body is meant for my body, and there's something special about taking care of myself in a special way.

KOLE, age thirteen.
I like being able to be way more energetic at everything I do because I am an athlete and it helps a lot being plant-based.

These days, Ann's bright light and humor show up in our books, YouTube videos, and cooking demos. When we began presenting cooking demos decades ago, we had no idea we were *working* because it felt so natural—mother and daughter chatting, bickering, and laughing side by side. What's most gratifying is hearing from people who decide to try cooking plant-based because Ann makes them laugh, or because our relationship reminds them of their mother-daughter relationship, or we just make it look easy. It is so simple—and transformative—to embrace the power each of us has in our own kitchen.

My parents feel being plant-based is the greatest gift they will ever give to our family—the benefits of a lifestyle-related disease-free life will extend for generations to come. We hope this book will inspire you to protect your family's health, too, and make food choices that also nourish the planet! Be tenacious in your drive to change the world around you, whether it's by chatting with interested pals, barking behind a bullhorn, or being a silent role model. Set the example and make yourself a resource. Choose to be fierce, and roar for your own health!

Becoming a Plant-Based Woman Warrior
From Ann:

I grew up eating city pigeons, which my father called quail; snails off the driveway after a rain, which, of course, my father called escargot; abalone that we caught ourselves and pounded until tender and fried; and roadkill my father found still warm with a gleam in its eye. And the Criles, my family, were famous for our goat roasts, often made with the head of the goat crowned and ruffled on a spike over a firepit. We even had a goat roast the night before my husband and I were married sixty years ago.

The following is a handwritten guest and menu record:

Where given **THE KNOB**

Date Aug. 1951.

Occasion ANNUAL **GOAT ROAST**

Guests Present

Hales, Don & Marion
Tunbulls, Dougie & Ryza
Effers, Don & Joanna
K reigers,
Moores, 2
Robinett,
Crofts, 6
Siffers,
King, Solly, 1
Michek,
Aides,
Buchon, 1
Leidens, Sa
McKee, 1
Rameys,
Gonzettons, 1
Scheids
Perkins, 1
Kings
Guenes,
Glasnens,

Unable to Attend

Menu

Tijuana Salad :
30 heads of Romainishe
(wore few enoys)
Corn - roasted in fire
6 dz. (need 2 apiece)
GOATS : Two (wine for sewing)
stuffed 2 woodchicks
(boil 1/2 hr + brown first)
BARBEQUE SAUCE
SPONGE CAKE : 6 large, 2 small
(coneep)
Coffee : (should be thos cafe or
made at time in basket)
Peanuts :

Wines
1/4 BEER - Schlitz (need 1 1/2)
4 BOURBON
2 SCOTCH
(6 cases - Schlitz - extra)

Table Decorations
1 Goat Head on spike —
Crowned & Truffled

Soon after Essy and I married in 1961, the first fancy dinner we served for our land-lords and my parents was TONGUE. Beef tongue! Today I can't conceive of serving that or how it's even possible to swallow it.

Around this time, my father, George Crile Jr., was a general surgeon and an out-of-the-box thinker. He challenged the radical mastectomy as a treatment for breast cancer, arguing that it was an extreme and disfiguring operation that was no better a cure for cancer than less invasive procedures. He also lived life fully. He and my mother, Jane Halle Crile, invented a way to take underwater photography (using a rebreather bag from the operating room!) at the same time as Cousteau, and they lectured around the world. They dove for treasure and wrote a book about their journeys called *Treasure Diving Holidays*. The cover featured all six of us children standing backward in yellow turtlenecks and black tights with frightening faces painted on our rears to "scare away the sharks." We had a childhood of adventure, and we continued to eat from our environ-ment. It was the way it was.

But that was then, a lifetime far away.

In 1982, my husband, Essy, a general surgeon at the Cleveland Clinic who also worked with cancer patients, finally grew tired of operating on women with breast cancer and dedicated himself to finding a preventative cure. Looking globally, he

saw that women in Japan, who ate a largely plant-based diet, rarely had breast cancer. In contrast, when Japanese families immigrated to the United States, second and third generation Japanese American women had the same rate of breast cancer as their Caucasian counterparts. He decided to do a study on diet but felt that if he did a generational study on women, he would be long dead before it was finished. So, he chose to work with heart disease patients.

At this point, Essy announced he was no lon-ger eating *any* meat or any dairy. He felt if he was going to ask patients to eat this way, he had to do it also. And so there I was: a full-time teacher with four children in their early to mid teens, with *no* time and *no* idea how to cook a new way. We knew no one who ate plant-based. There was no inter-net, no endless vegan recipe books. And *no* support other than our imagination. But we did it. We fig-ured it out.

It gave us a wonderful spirit of togetherness to eat a whole food, plant-based diet along with Essy's research patients. Almost immediately, the benefits of plant-based nutrition for reversing his patients' heart disease became clear. And just as swiftly, we became convinced a plant-based diet was the healthiest way forward for us as well.

We praised the day our children switched to plant-based. Fortunately, each of their spouses fully embraces plant-based eating. And, of course, the food at their weddings featured rice and beans or plant-based lasagna (no more goat roasts!). Without question, plant-based eating is the best gift we have given our children, and in turn, our grandchildren.

I feel so fortunate to have discovered whole food, plant-based nutrition and the excitement of helping others live healthier lives through the power of food. Jane and I hear stories from people daily about the dramatic transformations they have experienced after changing to a plant-based diet: increased energy, reversal of diabetes and heart disease, weight loss, and more. Today, when I see hamburger and chicken in grocery carts, I have to stop myself from lecturing absolute strangers about the power of plant-based eating!

The well-worn pine needle path between our houses has been one of our greatest joys. It gives us the opportunity to be a part of the lives of our grandchildren and the recipients of so much good food—but above all, it's given us such a special, daily friendship.

When the bells on our door jingle, our response is Pavlovian: "Jane's here!" Inevitably, she's arrived with a sample of her latest creation. For a month, we were the lucky recipients of her Outta Sight Brownies. We liked every version, but on the tenth warm, moist brownie trial, we knew she had hit the jackpot. You're going to love them, too (page 297). Honestly, we are amazed that somehow we continue to discover delicious flavors and recipes, and our collection of favorite recipes keeps growing! It makes it easy to stay on the plant-based path, and we get so excited to share them with others. We hope these recipes will find a delicious spot in your home, too.

CHAPTER 1

HOW PLANTS POWERFULLY SUPPORT WOMEN

No matter where you are on the plant-based path—whether you started yesterday, ten years ago, or plan to start tomorrow—welcome! Being a Plant-Based Woman Warrior is about being a part of a community, and we want to meet you wherever you are. As you'll read in this chapter and the "Becoming a Woman Warrior" stories, this is a lifestyle of hope and longevity. Eating plants boosts every aspect of a woman's health, not just physically but emotionally, too.

There is no "winning" in this community—just our united goal of eating plants in support of our bodies, the health of others, and our planet. Our intent is to share our process, one based on vitality, community, and good energy—not perfectionism. We want to stride together toward health and nourishment and away from rules, rigidity, restriction, and judgment.

Finding Food Freedom

Food is tricky. Especially for us women. For some of us, the nuanced food landscape is, at best, confusing. And for others, it becomes a continuous challenge, one that reveals unhealthy patterns: orthorexia, anorexia, bulimia, and binge-eating disorder.

We have witnessed these unhealthy patterns in family, friends, and loved ones who too tightly embrace guidelines as if they have a life-threatening disease, like heart disease, when they do not. Restrictions and rules around food trigger some of us in health-threatening ways.

Do not confuse being a Plant-Based Woman Warrior with perfectionism. We are all imperfect. We are all flawed. We are all on a path. This is a process. If our plant-based guidelines trigger a troubling urge to rigidly restrict yourself, please consider speaking with someone or seeking professional help.

For me (Jane), I shudder to think how weary-worn and lost I would be today without discovering plant-based eating. It has offered a freedom from a path of chronic food and body hang-ups.

Growing up, my brothers and I were all crazy-skinny kids. Once I hit adolescence, though, I started filling out, while my brothers did not. By my late teens, I was a super-fit, nationally ranked swimmer frustrated about my weight and curves. Every day, this mind-body thought virus occupied swaths of my time. I envied my brothers, who did not squander even a moment on such concerns.

I remember preparing to go on a trip with one of my brothers and his friends. One of his pals showed up wearing a T-shirt with a chicken on it surrounded by a red circle with a line through it. The T-shirt said, "No Fat Chicks." Something snapped in me—I hid under my mom's desk flooded with feelings I could not understand. I couldn't think straight. "I have fat on my body. Am I a fat chick? How could he wear that shirt?" I kept wondering. I didn't feel comfortable being around him or that energy, so I ended up not going on that trip. I hope no one ever goes on trips with anyone who broadcasts or cultivates that kind of toxic message.

Food is so much more than just fuel, and navigating how to eat is a puzzle. One weekend in college my roommates and I decided the three of us had to eat a whole case (forty-eight) of Snickers bars in twenty-four hours. My friend Laurie still has the wrappers to prove it. Another weekend I

We
Plant-Based
WOMEN
WARRIORS

Eat plants.

Swim in open water.

Live with energy and spark.

Are imperfect.

Help friends move.

Do cartwheels—or try to!

Plant gardens.

Read.

Get it on.

Feed our microbiome.

Do handstands—or try to!

Ride bikes.

Take hikes.

Dance.

Prance.

Move our bowels.

Feel unbridled.

Believe the best is yet to come.

landed a chocolate-induced migraine, something I had not experienced since the seventh grade when I'd plowed through my pillowcase of Halloween candy in one night. Sure, I was a vegetarian at the time, but that doesn't mean I always made healthy choices.

Like each of us, I had to figure out how to move forward with food. That meant instead of grabbing french fries and Froyo, choosing baked potatoes and brown rice stir-fry. Learning that oatmeal in the morning instead of granola bars was not only cheaper, it also lasted longer in my belly.

Splurging on birthday cake, Nutella, or junk food with friends came with accurate feedback from my body: rotten sleep patterns, low energy, and cravings for more junk. My bowels also sent clear messages by turning to stone or raging like a river. After college, I found sticking with a plant-based diet made me feel better head to toe.

Soon enough, I began to feel more comfortable with my food choices, my body, and myself. What a blessed relief to not waste time on body-food thoughts. It felt like a luxury—a welcomed absence of that burdensome mindset many of us have around food. One of my friends created a term for this exhausting civil war: "food-head." For her, a plant-based diet removed the hulking, omnipresent concerns about weight and self-worth. Indeed, that has matched my experience. Plant-based eating released me from a mind laden with body- and food-based preoccupations. If I had not found a plant-based diet, what would the toll have been on my body and identity? I feel so *wicked* lucky that I do not know.

I am grateful beyond measure to be a Plant-Based Woman Warrior.

Protecting Against Lifestyle Diseases

We do not mean to do it, but sometimes we make ourselves sick. Lifestyle-related diseases develop because we have eaten, smoked, or otherwise lifestyled ourselves into a disease state—with the assistance of too little sleep, too much inactivity, and loads of stress. The American College of Lifestyle Medicine, a new, board-certified branch of medicine, identifies six evidence-based lifestyle therapeutic interventions, the first and most impactful being a plant-based diet. The other pillars are regular exercise, restorative sleep, stress management, no smoking, and positive social connections. The ACLM puts the focus on a plant-based diet to lead the charge against type 2 diabetes, heart disease, and multiple types of preventable cancers. Find a practitioner who is ACLM certified, or ask that your practitioner become ACLM certified.

Type 2 Diabetes

Type 2 diabetes is not a malignancy. One cannot catch it from someone else. So, how does it develop? There are three major players involved: glucose (blood sugar), insulin (the transporter of glucose), and muscle cells (which use glucose). And there is one scoundrel: dietary fats. Our stomach breaks food down into glucose, and then our insulin molecules load up with glucose and transport it to our muscle cells. It works beautifully. It gets tricky only when the dietary fats show up.

In a healthy person's body, part of the insulin molecule perfectly inserts itself in the muscle cell like a charger into a phone or a car into a tight garage. It is then able to deliver the glucose inside the cell, allowing a person to carry on with energy, attention, vim, and vigor.

But when there is too much dietary fat in one's system, a fatty buildup called intramyocellular lipid blocks this perfect insert so the insulin molecule cannot dock on and deliver glucose to the muscle cell. The muscle cells have become insulin resistant and the glucose remains in the blood, which is known as high blood sugar.

But luckily, this malfunction is akin to autumn leaves blocking your gutter or hair clogging the shower drain—it can be reversed. Adopting a whole food, plant-based lifestyle will clear off the fatty buildup on the muscle cells and allow the insulin to drop off the glucose once again.

(To learn more about diabetes, we suggest *Dr. Neal Barnard's Program for Reversing Diabetes* by Neal D. Barnard, MD, or *Mastering Diabetes* by Cyrus Khambatta and Robby Barbaro. For an explanatory video, check out "The Power of Plants to Prevent and Reverse Type 2 Diabetes" on Jane's YouTube channel.)

There is only one dietary source of cholesterol: animal products.

When you eat a whole food, plant-based diet, your meals are high in fiber and low in fat. You do not eat animal products, and so you do not consume any dietary cholesterol. The endothelial cells, free from the punishing blow of grease, meat, cheese, and dairy, remain healthy and free of lifestyle-related vascular issues. Even adopting a plant-based diet later in life can reverse the impact of a more standard American diet. (For more on heart disease and plant-based nutrition, please see *Prevent and Reverse Heart Disease* by C. B. Esselstyn Jr., MD, or *How Not to Die* by Michael Greger, MD.)

Becoming a Plant-Based Woman Warrior

PATRICIA

I had a love affair with food most of my life, and I was absolutely addicted to sugar, processed foods, and animal products. By the time I was fifty-eight, I was suffering from obesity, diabetes, arthritis, and severe heart disease. I was at least one hundred pounds overweight for most of my life, yet my body was starving nutritionally. I was clueless when it came to nutrition.

In 2007, I was diagnosed with type 2 diabetes, and my blood sugar was an incredible 441. I started experiencing shortness of breath and angina pain in my jaw and left arm. As a result, I had five coronary artery bypasses in 2008: two arteries were 100 percent occluded, two were 90 percent, and one was 80 percent. Doctors never informed me that my disease was progressive, and I thought they had "fixed" me. Upon discharge from the hospital, I was taking thirteen pills and receiving two shots a day. I was told to eat the Mediterranean diet, to limit my carbohydrates, and avoid potatoes, rice, bread, and pasta. My diabetes was never really controlled because I never understood my sugar addiction.

In February 2014, after experiencing angina almost every day since my heart surgery, I was admitted to the Cleveland Clinic for an angiogram to evaluate the status of my coronary artery bypasses. As a result, they had to insert seven stents into my arteries, and one week later upon emergency readmission, they inserted an eighth stent into an artery that was 90 percent occluded. Upon my release from the hospital, they told me that I had severe heart disease and all my arteries were at least 50 percent blocked—even my bypasses—and they warned me that I would be back in the hospital within six months with yet another cardiac event.

Needless to say, I was overwhelmed and depressed. I cried for days! Shortly thereafter, I started having daily angina pain again, so I called my cardiologist. She told me that she could prescribe a nitroglycerin patch to ease my pain. I knew right then that they could not "fix" me. They also did a blood test for a genetic component,

LP(a), which is associated with heart disease. I did test somewhat positive for LP(a), so now we could blame my health condition on my genetics, instead of me taking any responsibility for my health situation, such as my destructive eating habits. We rely too much on another pill or procedure to save us from what we have created, right at the end of our forks, every day, over decades.

In the middle of the night, depressed and crying out, "Oh God, please help me, don't let me die, please show me the way!," I started researching on the internet how to stop the progression of heart disease. I found Dr. Esselstyn's book *Prevent and Reverse Heart Disease*. I read it from cover to cover and committed to the whole food, plant-based (WFPB) lifestyle overnight! I called Dr. Esselstyn's office, and he returned my call, assuring me that it was in fact what I was eating every day that had completely destroyed my endothelial cells, which had led to my heart disease. He told me a WFPB lifestyle trumps genetics, and he gave me hope when I had none!

Within two weeks, my daily angina stopped completely! Next thing I knew, I was not sleeping all afternoon as I had done for years. Then, I started walking daily and was totally committed to this lifestyle. I was on a mission to save my life! Within a short period of time, God (and a few whole food, plant-based doctors) had shown me the way! I began to come off some of my medications, starting with one diabetic pill, then a blood pressure pill, and so on. My joints stopped aching . . . and there went another pill!

It has been over six years, and I have not fulfilled the dire forecast that I would have another cardiac event within six months; in fact, I feel better than I have in over twenty years!

Remember those thirteen pills and two shots daily? No more shots, and I take only a small dose of a statin. Why? Because the medical community will *not* take you off statin drugs when you have known heart disease, even though my total cholesterol is only 96. Gone are the days of angina, diabetes, arthritis, neuropathy in my feet, high blood pressure, sugar cravings, and weight issues. I have lost at least one hundred pounds, and I have maintained my weight. I don't weigh or measure any food; plus, I eat until I am satisfied.

Cancer

Eating to save your heart and prevent diabetes also decreases your cancer risk. A plant-based diet helps the natural process of apoptosis, or cell death—the killing off of unhealthy cells like cancer cells. And while the consumption of animal products has been shown to increase the promotion of cancer, a plant-based diet has been shown to fight off cancer cells. In the next section, we touch on the protective effect of plants against breast cancer specifically.

(For more on cancer and plant-based eating, we suggest *How Not to Die* by Michael Greger, MD, and *The China Study* by T. Colin Campbell.)

Supporting Hormonal and Sexual Health

The power, blessings, and beauty of being a woman are endless—as are some of the burdens that come with being a woman: menstrual issues, fertility challenges, menopause symptoms, breast health, and uterine health. One of the main players in all the above is estrogen. Estrogen makes us women. We love it and we need it—until, like a houseguest who has overstayed their welcome, we no longer do.

Our bodies produce all the estrogen we need: cholesterol + fat = estrogen. If we eat animal-based foods, we consume extra estrogen. And increasing our estrogen levels causes trouble. According to Dr. Kristi Funk, breast cancer doctor and author of *Breasts: The Owner's Manual*, the *quantity* of estrogen matters because 80 percent of breast cancer is fed by estrogen.

Becoming a Plant-Based Woman Warrior

LILY

I had been having really strong, really frequent hot flashes for more than two years. They were so strong, they sometimes hurt all day and night, and at night they completely interrupted my sleep. Two days into the [plant-based] diet, they stopped. Gone. Very occasionally I will get like a small wave of heat, but I don't break a sweat and hardly notice it. I sleep through the night now. Amazing. I feel so grateful. The only problem is now I want to change the world. I want to proselytize in a way I've never wanted to proselytize before—not about literature or climate change or anything else I feel passionate about, but about the power of a plant-based diet.

In addition, excess estrogen can also cause menstrual issues and fibroids to grow in the uterus. Fibroids are like stalactites in a cave—they hang on to the uterine lining and grow larger. They can cause severe bleeding even if they are small, which can lead to anemia. Sadly, some physicians address symptoms of fibroids by performing a hysterectomy, that is, removing a woman's uterus, when just removing dairy from her diet may be all that is needed. (See *Your Body in Balance* by Neal D. Barnard, MD.)

The one-two punch of it is, animal products are not only high in estrogen but also low in fiber. This means that as meat and dairy slowly make their way through our intestines, we absorb more and more estrogen for as long as it takes to pass through our system.

On the other hand, phytoestrogens—plant-based estrogens—are protective against tumors of the breast. Here's why: We have alpha and beta receptors in the breast. Our own estrogen stimulates the alpha receptors, which signal cancer cells to grow. Yet, when phytoestrogens land on beta receptors of the breast, they act like umbrellas blocking estrogen's access to the alpha receptors. In other words, our breasts love plants, and plants love our breasts.

Numerous Indigenous cultures do not have a word for menopause because historically and culturally it does not exist. These cultures primarily consume a diet based on plants. The path to menopause tends to be gentle on a plant-based diet—natural

Becoming a Plant-Based Woman Warrior

JORDI

I was a recently married twenty-five-year-old experiencing heavy menstrual bleeding and constant uterine pain. My gynecologist performed an endometrial ablation, but it didn't improve my symptoms, so she sent me to a local reproductive endocrinologist and infertility specialist who recommended yet another ablation and dilation and curettage (D&C). Immediately following the second procedure, he informed me it was not effective due to multiple large uterine fibroids, which were essentially filling my uterus. His only recommendation was a complete hysterectomy. I was an otherwise healthy young woman, and he explained to me that I would never be able to conceive, and if I did, I certainly would not be able to carry the baby to term. He offered no hope whatsoever.

My parents had been whole food, plant-based for several years, and after much encouragement from them, I decided to try plant-based nutrition as an alternative because I refused to believe a hysterectomy was my only option. I never thought I wanted a baby until I was told I couldn't have one.

In the meantime, I found another physician specializing in female reproductive abnormalities. After just a short time eating plant-based, the fibroids had become barely visible! I underwent robotic surgery to remove the fibroids, which required very little attention.

Almost exactly one year to the day after starting a plant-based diet and being told "You will never be able to conceive," I gave birth to a wonderful, healthy little "miracle boy"! Eighteen months later, I became pregnant with my second child, a beautiful, healthy girl!

estrogen and hormonal adjustments are mild or even imperceptible compared to what women who eat hormonal meat and dairy products experience.

Let's move on to sex. If this were a book for Plant-Based Men Warriors, there would be numerous chapters on sex, sexual health, and sexual pleasure. We are not going to miss this opportunity to at least address it briefly!

A surprising number of women are not in tune with their own anatomy. The old-school model of teaching female reproductive anatomy from the front view is complicated. It looks like a graceful insect in a bodybuilding contest.

Through teaching middle school sex ed for decades, I discovered the most comprehensive way to discuss female reproductive anatomy is summed up in the acronym CUVA: clitoris, urethra, vagina, anus. It's a more practical way of thinking of the whole pelvic floor, front to back. I have found the CUVA perspective clarifies that the function, purpose, and potential of a woman's sexual body parts are equal to a man's. As a society we are familiar with a male's penis and its capacity to perform urination, reproduction, and sexual pleasure. Most people don't realize that a woman's vulva (the proper term for CUVA) also has the capacity for urination, reproduction, and sexual pleasure, just in separate areas.

If we were taught this from the start, would there be more equality around our sexuality and identity? Would it be easier to be a strong and fierce woman from the get-go? Indeed. I have found the CUVA perspective clarifies that our function, purpose, and potential are equal, no matter how this has been previously hidden or misunderstood. How is a whole food, plant-based diet CUVA's friend and protector? In so many beautiful ways!

First things first, C, the clitoris. This pleasure center hosts eight thousand nerves for sexual pleasure. When the clitoris is stimulated, this conductor of bliss benefits from increased blood flow, resulting in external as well as internal engorgement of the crura and vestibular bulb tissue. The latter is the same tissue found in the shaft of the penis. And like the penis, this tissue responds to stimulus by engorging with blood. This natural, healthy response occurs when the endothelial layer within the arteries releases nitric oxide and dilates—increasing blood flow. And what does a plant-based diet increase? Blood flow. Lubrication is also made of plasma from the blood flow, an adequate amount of nitric oxide from healthy endothelial cells, and estrogen. We get emails from women all the time about their sex lives, with bawdy stories about their renewed drive and incredible orgasms. Some attribute this new spark to feeling better in their own bodies, and others credit their blood flow reaching new and exciting places. (For more about healthier endothelium and increased blood flow in arteries, please see *Prevent and Reverse Heart Disease* by C. B. Esselstyn Jr., MD.)

And then, U, the urethra. A plant-based diet supports the urinary tract by reducing the harmful effects of animal foods, particularly poultry. Chicken appears to serve as a reservoir for antibiotic-resistant E. coli, correlated with urinary tract infections (UTIs). Less chicken equals fewer UTIs, fewer bladder infections, and fewer kidney issues. (For more on this topic, we suggest *How Not to Die* by Michael Greger, MD.)

Next, *V*, the vagina. Vaginal health is supported by healthy blood flow to help with circulation and lubrication. Our organs above the vagina, that is, our uterus and ovaries, are also protected by eating plants over animal foods as they help dodge fibroids, anemia, cancers, and possible unnecessary hysterectomies. (See Jordi's story, page 30. And for more information on these topics, we suggest *Your Body in Balance* by Neal D. Barnard, MD.)

And bringing up the rear, *A*, the anus. Above the anus are our bowels. Eating plants is a moving experience! Bowels love fiber. Plants are filled with fiber. Consuming plant-based fiber makes our bowels move with ease, so constipation is not an issue. The lack of constipation helps prevent hemorrhoids and diverticulitis as well.

Boosting Immunity

A massive amount of our immune system lives in the essential bacteria and microbes in our gut and our bowels, which is called our microbiome. There is a great deal of talk lately about taking probiotics for gut health, but the best bang for your buck is to eat high-fiber foods. And fiber is found only in plants. When our microbiome consumes fiber, the process creates a powerful by-product called short-chain fatty acids, which are anti-inflammatory and anti-cancer. To ensure the proliferation of these healthy microbes and bacteria in our microbiome, we *must* eat fiber.

When we consume a diet heavy in meat, dairy, or oil, the kind of bacteria our microbiome uses to break down these foods does not make anti-inflammatory short-chain fatty acids. Rather, these unhealthy microbes cause you to crave *more* meat, dairy, and oil in order to keep themselves alive.

Our microbiome is strengthened by the variety and volume of plants we consume daily. (For more information on the microbiome and gut health, we suggest *The Microbiome Solution* by Robynne Chutkan and *Fiber Fueled* by Will Bulsiewicz, MD.)

Becoming a Plant-Based Woman Warrior

JOYCE

I battled illness my entire life, literally from the day I was born. By the time I reached my thirties, lupus had filled my life with hospitalizations and cocktails of medications. Although the medications were increased annually, the lupus continued to progress, attacking all systems and organs of my body. In my early forties, bones disintegrated in my jaw, requiring reconstruction. I suffered from multiple daily seizures, debilitating neuropathy, and damage to my veins, lungs, heart, and kidneys. I was undergoing monthly infusions, but I was getting worse and was told I would require additional reconstruction surgery and had only a few years to live.

I was being placed on disability and losing driving privileges when I learned how others had conquered their illnesses simply by consuming a whole food, plant-based diet. I had always said I would try anything to stop lupus, so I took a leap of faith. I stopped having seizures within days and began decreasing medications the first month. Within five years, my kidneys had fully repaired, and I was 100 percent free of all lupus medications. Since then, I have adopted an intense workout regimen and have completed numerous physical challenges and indoor triathlons. In my fifties, I am the healthiest and strongest I have ever been. I am not only alive, I thrive.

I have been given a second chance at life because I learned that we really should "let food be thy medicine and medicine be thy food."

As a Plant-Based Woman Warrior, you set yourself up to be a healthy woman inside and out with increased blood flow, resistance to lifestyle diseases, a strong immune system, and a supple digestive system. Plus, you feel truly comfortable in your body. Cheers to that!

Becoming a Plant-Based Woman Warrior

SARAY

Learning I had multiple sclerosis at age twenty-eight felt like the end, literally. It seemed life was over.

A leading MS doctor broke the bad news: "You will likely be in a wheelchair in ten to twenty years." That's all I heard, then came the stream of tears after what felt like a kick to the gut. Was this it for me? After all the hard work and sacrifice to achieve my dream of becoming a physician myself, this is how my life would end?

I decided I would do all the doctors asked of me; I would be a good and compliant patient. This meant daily injections of the most recently approved treatment to slow the progression of the disease and an additional dozen drugs to manage symptoms and side effects. But life only got harder. Over the years that followed, it was a building pattern of more pain, more fatigue, more depression, more insomnia, and more weakness, and I was only in my early thirties. How much more of this could I sustain? Despair took over and hope was lost. Then, at the darkest moment came the shine of the brightest light.

In 2003, I read an article that introduced the concept of diet and its effects on MS. I was skeptical but unabashedly curious. I took a deep dive into the scientific literature to learn as much as I could about how diet could affect disease. What I found was literally life changing. It was indeed true that diet and optimal lifestyle could prevent, manage, and even reverse disease states. I was eager to get started on this new journey, equipped with powerful peer-reviewed scientific evidence as my compass.

The first step I took was adopting a whole food, plant-based diet. After years of a sedentary lifestyle, largely because of bad advice, disability, and dependence on a cane, I began to exercise regularly. I learned how to sleep in the absence of pills and practiced daily prayer and meditation to address my stress. I embraced and fortified meaningful relationships with my close family and friends. I focused on the positives rather than the negatives. I smiled more and expressed gratitude more frequently.

My story has a happy ending, but that didn't come overnight. It took months and years to revert from a weak, disabled, dependent, chronic disease patient to a fully functional medication- and disability-free physician. In 2010, seven years after I opted to consume plants over animals and processed junk, I ran a marathon.

Today, now more than twenty-five years since my MS diagnosis, I remain well and impassioned to share the power of plants with all who are ready to receive it. My second goal is to bring awareness to physicians across the globe, so I embarked on the making of a documentary film, *Code Blue*. I hope the film's lessons will serve to create a movement in medicine to place greater emphasis on prevention by teaching doctors the importance of nutrition and lifestyle on disease formation. We can produce a new era in clinical medicine that will lead to a dramatic reduction in chronic diseases, build hospitals and clinics that embody the principles of prevention by serving plant-based foods, and create physicians who, too, practice what they preach and serve as incontrovertible examples for their patients.

Today, I am free of pharmaceuticals and stand tall on my own two feet. In 1995, they said I'd be wheelchair bound by now. I'm so glad to have proved them wrong.

Becoming a Plant-Based Woman Warrior

MONICA

Nine years ago, when my third child, Asha, was born, I was a full-time cardiologist, a wife of twelve years, and a mother of three children under four and two fur babies. Soon, I started manifesting migratory joint pain that took me from being an avid runner to being unable to climb the stairs. In a matter of weeks from symptom onset, I was diagnosed with a chronic, debilitating form of rheumatoid arthritis. I was told that there was no cure for this illness and that my inflammatory markers suggested a poor long-term prognosis. I was told that I needed to get used to being on medications for the rest of my life. Nothing prepares you for illness. In fact, for someone like myself who likes—*who needs*—to be in control, such an illness can be life shattering. I went through the multiple stages of guilt and anger that come with such a defining moment. I was angry that I got sick (*Why me?*) and that I had tempted fate in having a third child (*If I hadn't had a third child, I would have been okay, right?*). I was left with an emptiness and fear that I would have every side effect from the medications I was on, that I would be handicapped with three small kids, and that my life was completely out of my control. The hardest thing I did was stop nursing my baby. The medications would have carried through to the breast milk, so the doctor told me I had to stop nursing and I needed to get on medications within a week. I did what I needed to do and stopped. I can still taste the salt from my tears as I walked away when the baby started crying and I couldn't feed her.

As I went on medications and started feeling like myself, I became a student again—learning all about autoimmune disease. I studied how the disease works, what triggers it, and how the medications work. I also learned about the microbiome, leaky gut, and lifestyle modifications that improve gut integrity. I was blown away learning about how much of autoimmune disease seems related to leaky gut and how the integrity of the gut can be affected by stress and poor nutrition. After extensive study, I took a leap of faith and I decided then to change everything: I started doing yoga and learned to meditate to reduce stress. I slept more and learned, most importantly, how to eat. I eliminated a lot of foods. For me, I believe, dairy was an inflammatory trigger. I started eating whole, unrefined, plant-based foods. I learned about anti-inflammatory foods and spices and incorporated them all in. About a year after I started changing my lifestyle, I started weaning off my drugs. I am proud to note that I have been off all medications for over six years, without any signs of inflammation. I am back to being a running fiend, but I also focus on yoga, Pilates, and movement in general. I eat right every day. I sleep and work on reducing stress. People often ask, "Don't you find you cheat a lot?" The truth is, I don't. I have been so sick before. I was disabled and unable to walk. I couldn't button my baby's clothes or even lift her up. I will *never* go back to eating poorly, nor will I ever ignore the signals that my body gives me about needing more sleep or having too much stress.

I changed my whole practice of cardiology and built a preventive cardiology program at an academic university hospital, working with patients and teaching the next generation of physicians about the importance of nutrition, lifestyle, and health. I am proud of the changes I have made and more importantly, I am thankful for what my body gives me every day. When I had Asha and got sick, I blamed her. I had a lot of anger and sadness. But the funny thing is that Asha didn't make me sick; she saved me. Over and over again, that little child of mine surprises me. And that has made all the difference.

CHAPTER 2

CREATE
DELICIOUS

Delicious food wins people over to plant-based eating better than any weaponry in our arsenal. What's the best way to learn to make delicious food? Spend time in your own kitchen. It is the most important room in the home.

We are bold and brave in the kitchen, which means we are willing to be adventurers and totally mess up. We are masters at failing and trying anew. For example, no one would eat the millet and rice flour muffins that I worked hard to develop for this book. I finally poked them into the bird feeder for the birds and squirrels, and they wouldn't even eat them either! Yet that same recipe did lead us to the Seed and Millet Crackers (page 203), which is a winner.

When you cook with creativity, you can make new food traditions in your kitchen. Black beans and brown rice with loads of toppings is our favorite on Christmas Eve, and no birthday party is complete without artichokes. Occasionally, we reboot old favorites like the newest version of Our Chocolate Cake with German Chocolate Frosting (pages 301, 308) when we want to show off, and Amaretto Cherry Chocolate Hazelnut Scones (page 291) when an army of kids arrives after swim practice. We feel strongly that eating plant-based does not mean depriving yourself of the pleasures of eating. A few months into this cookbook project, we knew we were on the right path when our recipes tally stood at ten breakfasts, eight lunches, and forty-four desserts. Right on target!

Becoming a Plant-Based Woman Warrior

CHAR

While it seems like yesterday, it was actually Wednesday, September 23, 2009, in Rockville, Maryland. While working for Whole Foods Market, I had gone to a meeting where our regional president told us about *The Engine 2 Diet* and the book's author, Rip Esselstyn. While our leader had lost weight, what I noticed most was a change in his demeanor and the perfect appearance of his skin. I was sold. "Who doesn't want perfect skin," I thought.

Every day of this plant-based challenge was a test for me—figuring out the next meals to make. I kept a running list of the foods I would eat on the twenty-ninth day (when the challenge was over). The list is sickening to me now—high in fat, salt, and calories. I now see them as "disease contributors" and they carry zero appeal. But, on the tenth day of the Engine 2 Challenge, when I woke up, I noticed that for the first time in years, I was free of my crippling osteoarthritis pain. I had been managing terrible pain by taking over-the-counter pain relievers but was never pain-free. Since becoming plant-based, I rarely take anything for pain, because I basically live a pain-free life.

On that tenth day, I remember thinking, "Food is medicine." The twenty-ninth day finally arrived, but it involved more leafy greens, whole grains, and legumes. The recipes in Rip's book were delicious, easy to make and follow. Two things dropped: my grocery bills and my weight. I think I was tipping the scales at nearly three hundred pounds.

Six months after jumping into the plant-strong pool, I attended the inaugural Engine 2 Immersion in Austin, Texas. When I met Ann and Jane, I thought that my heart was going to skip a beat. I attended every cooking seminar they taught—sitting in the front row so as not to miss a minute of their recipe ideas. I also felt a certain joy from their banter and humor. Their joy was infectious, but in my heart I felt this message of "You can do this."

For me, weight is not the most significant element of being plant-based. I live a prescription-free life, I have zero disease conditions, and even at the age of seventy, I lead a productive and active life. Being plant-based redirected my life and gave me more purpose. I teach nutrition and plant-based cooking in underserved pockets of Philadelphia. I often wonder what my life would be like had I never gone to that meeting in Rockville. Heart disease and cancer run in my family, and I push hard every day to make certain that I maximize my plant-based potential to be the best version of myself that I can be.

There is a great saying from the twelve-step world: "Take what you want and leave the rest behind." We are all given many choices and chances in our lives, and for me, eating plants has provided me with the best fodder for healthy living that I can imagine.

Food as Medicine

My kitchen feels like the bridge of the starship *Enterprise*—I'm the captain in charge, directing and protecting my family's health. Over the years, my husband, Brian, and I have watched our kids form habits that will last them a lifetime. Seeing them prefer pizza with no cheese, morning oats, and Buddha bowls filled with tempeh, beans, and greens makes our hearts sing and keeps their hearts healthy!

Investing mere minutes into cooking your own plant-based food translates directly to adding healthy years to your own life. Processed foods, packaged foods, prepared foods, and take-out food incessantly tempt us with their chemically achieved bliss point of sugar, salt, and fat. Bottom line, that food is prepared for you, not by you. And no matter what the box boasts or the commercial claims, they are not looking out for your health. Wendell Berry's famous quote nails it: "People are fed by the food industry, which pays no attention to health, and are treated by the health industry, which pays no attention to food."

Ann and I are hardwired to prepare food to prevent disease, which is reflected in the ingredients we use. We tend to cook with walnuts more often than other nuts due to their healthy omega-3 to omega-6 ratio. It's the same reason we often spoon flaxseed meal or chia seeds into our meals wherever possible. When we cook with turmeric, we try to include black pepper to help with bioavailability. (Ann votes for adding turmeric to everything, literally everything.) Arugula is our green of choice as it is best for boosting nitric oxide production, which is crucial to vascular health. And we sneak oranges, blueberries, mangoes, or tomatoes into our salads to be sure we get enough vitamin C, which helps mobilize iron into the blood. After a while, it all becomes habit.

While the focus of this cookbook is not squarely on reversing heart disease like much of our other work, loads of recipes adhere to those guidelines and we have labeled them as "heart disease–friendly" so that they are easy to find. We have also included heart-healthy substitutions in some recipes. Some recipes do use some avocado and nuts, which are not part of a plant-based diet for those with heart disease, but they are foods we enjoy on occasion. Honestly, the dessert section is our favorite as it has a *bazillion* more recipes than the dessert chapters in our other books!

Our Plant-Based Woman Warrior Guidelines:

- No meat
- No dairy
- No added oil
- Minimal salt
- Minimal sweet

No meat is easy, no dairy is easy. And we unflinchingly adhere to our "no added oil" rule because, full pun intended, it is a slippery slope. Once you start using oil, you just won't stop. We don't argue that the mouthfeel makes everything taste good, and it also makes dishes smell delicious as they sizzle and bake. But the momentary, external pleasure of oil is a wolf in sheep's clothing. As we mentioned earlier, oil consumption increases the risk for heart disease, type 2 diabetes, and obesity. We just don't use oil.

We also keep our salt use to a minimum. Salt preference is quite personal, and it's an ingredient that is easy to adjust. In our kitchens, we tend to use low-sodium tamari, which is like soy sauce, while some of our PBWW pals are quick to grab liquid aminos—either is fine. Most often, when we list salt in our ingredients lists, we indicate that it is optional or to taste.

Sweetness is similarly subjective and easy to tweak. We try our best to use maple syrup, fruit, or dates for sweetening. Some desserts can be heavy on maple syrup, we know, but we consider these to be occasional treats. There are some ingredients in our recipes, such as ketchup, barbecue sauce, hoisin sauce, and pickled ginger, that contain plain old sugar, which we prefer to high-fructose corn syrup. We use condiments sparingly, and we suggest you look for ones that ideally do not have sugar listed as the first ingredient on the label.

After finishing each of our cookbooks, collectively five so far, we can never imagine being able to create another recipe! But just like women, the delicious world of plants continues to deliver. Onward with plants, love, and each other, you strong, fierce, delicious Plant-Based Women Warriors!

CHAPTER 3

THE PLANT-BASED WOMAN WARRIOR KITCHEN

What's best to have in the fridge? A whole produce stand! We aim for always having a colorful variety of fresh greens, vegetables, fruit, berries, and mushrooms. The best produce for you is the produce you eat!

But in addition to an abundance of beautiful plants, you'll want to have cooking staples like tofu, tempeh, beans, whole-grain flours, spices, and more. Here is what we almost always have on hand in our Plant-Based Woman Warrior kitchen:

continues

Pantry and Fridge Staples

- Oats: steel-cut and old-fashioned rolled

- Brown rice: short grain, long grain, jasmine, basmati

- Black rice

- Quinoa: red, white, black, and tricolored

- Farro

- Polenta/grits/cornmeal

- Barley

- Sweet potatoes

- Yukon Gold potatoes

- Tiny/new potatoes

- Whole-grain pastas and noodles: whole wheat, brown rice, black rice ramen (we prefer Lotus Foods brand), lentil, garbanzo

- Whole-grain bread with no oil or added sugar: We prefer Ezekiel 4:9 brand breads, Alvarado St. Bakery No Salt Added Sprouted Multigrain Bread, or Silver Hills Bakery Heritage Grain Big Red's Bread

- Canned and dried beans: black, garbanzo, pinto, kidney, cannellini, red, lima, and navy

- Whole-grain flours: oat, chickpea, whole wheat, millet, corn, almond, and rye

- Shelf-stable silken tofu, firm and extra firm, for desserts

- Regular tofu (not shelf stable and should be refrigerated)

- Nuts: walnuts, pecans, cashews, pistachios, hazelnuts, peanuts

- Seeds: chia, flax, sesame, sunflower, pumpkin (Note: Flaxseed meal is not shelf stable and should be refrigerated.)

- Raisins: golden and dark

- Dates: We prefer Medjool

- Dairy-free chocolate chips

- Vegetable broth: We love PLANTSTRONG broths

- Tahini

- Nut butter: peanut, almond

- Oat milk: Pacific Foods brand original or Oatly (the one with no added oil!)

- Almond milk: unsweetened brands

- Soy milk: organic unsweetened brands with no added oils

- Baking powder: Hain's Featherweight with no sodium

Make Your Own Oat Flour

We use oat flour in a lot of recipes in this book. You can buy oat flour, or you can make it yourself at home! Simply blend 1 cup old-fashioned rolled oats in a high-speed blender to make ¾ cup oat flour.

Spices, Herbs, and Flavorful Condiments

Our kitchen would not be complete without spices and other delicious flavor boosters. Remember to use your spices when they are fresh for the most zing, and upgrade old bottles that are past their prime. Try new spices, too! Having the flavor weapons below in your arsenal will set you up to win the meal and win the day!

- ○ Oregano
- ○ Crushed rosemary
- ○ Thyme
- ○ Basil
- ○ Onion powder, minced onion
- ○ Garlic powder, garlic granules
- ○ Garam masala
- ○ Curry
- ○ Turmeric
- ○ Cinnamon
- ○ Nutmeg
- ○ Vanilla extract
- ○ Mint extract
- ○ Coconut extract

- ○ Ground cumin
- ○ Ground coriander
- ○ Ground cardamom
- ○ Lemon pepper: Mrs. Dash, McCormick, or Frontier brands
- ○ Trader Joe's Everything but the Bagel Sesame Seasoning Blend (Note: We love this blend, but you can make your own to control salt content.)
- ○ Cajun spice
- ○ Fresh cilantro
- ○ Fresh basil
- ○ Fresh parsley

- ○ Fresh garlic
- ○ Fresh ginger
- ○ Crystallized ginger
- ○ Sweet onions
- ○ Miso: mellow white, keep in fridge
- ○ Tamari: low-sodium or San-J brand Tamari Lite 50% Less Sodium
- ○ Barbecue sauce: Find a favorite, ideally one with no high-fructose corn syrup
- ○ Ketchup: Find a brand with no high-fructose corn syrup

- ○ Mustard, any of your favorites: stone-ground, yellow, Dijon, spicy brown, etc. Be sure to read the label to avoid added sugar, oil, mayonnaise, or eggs
- ○ Hot sauce, your favorite brand
- ○ 100 percent pure maple syrup
- ○ Nutritional yeast
- ○ Salsas, fresh or jarred, your favorite: Read labels to avoid added oil or excess salt
- ○ Vinegars: rice, apple cider, and high-quality balsamic (see below)

High-Quality Vinegars

We prefer high-quality balsamic vinegar from the Olive Tap, the Olive Scene, or California Balsamic. We are always slack-jawed at the myriad of choices. Explore the variety of flavors! Some of our favorites are the Olive Tap's 4 Leaf Quality, California Balsamic's Spice Traders Curry Balsamic, California Balsamic's Teriyaki Balsamic, the Olive Tap's Sicilian Lemon White, and the Olive Tap's Dark Chocolate Balsamic! They are definitely worth the investment as they bring so much incredible flavor to a dish.

HOW TO COOK SWEET POTATOES

Sweet potatoes are the foundation of many of our meals, and so we have a few ways we cook them depending on how much time we have: wrapped in foil and oven baked, microwaved, or just naked and boiled. Ann, who loves all types of sweet potatoes, declares baking in foil as the best way to prepare sweet potatoes.

Sweet potatoes, any number

TO BAKE WHOLE AND WRAPPED: When you are not in a hurry, you can't beat baking whole, unpeeled sweet potatoes.

Preheat the oven to 350°F. Wrap each sweet potato in foil and place it on the middle rack. Place a sheet pan under the potatoes, as juice may ooze out of them as they bake. Bake for an hour or more, depending on the size, until they are very soft to the touch. You will have incredibly moist sweet potatoes that nearly melt in your mouth.

TO BAKE WHOLE AND UNWRAPPED: Preheat the oven to 400°F. Line a sheet pan with parchment paper. Place any number of sweet potatoes on the parchment-lined pan and cook for 40 minutes to 1 hour, until soft throughout. Allow the sweet potatoes to cool a bit before serving. These will be moist and sweet and hold some structure.

TO BAKE SWEET POTATO CUBES: Preheat the oven to 400°F. Line a sheet pan with parchment paper. Chop your sweet potatoes into ½-inch cubes. Place the sweet potato cubes on the pan. Bake for 15 to 20 minutes, until the cubes are baked through and browned to your liking.

TO BOIL: Bring a large pot of water to a boil. If you are using a whole sweet potato, boil for 35 to 45 minutes, until soft in the center. If you are using 1-inch cubes of sweet potato, boil for 15 minutes, or until soft in the center.

TO MICROWAVE: When we need to hustle and get food cooked quickly, we call on Chef Mike (our trusty microwave). Pierce a medium sweet potato with a fork (so it doesn't explode). Place it in the microwave and cook for 8 minutes. If you are cooking more than one sweet potato, add 3 to 4 minutes per sweet potato. Give each sweet potato a squeeze to make sure it feels soft and cooked through. It is ready to be eaten whole, cubed, sliced, or mashed.

HOW TO COOK YUKON GOLD POTATOES

We cook Yukon Gold potatoes by the sack. Having cooked potatoes in the fridge ready to go is such a bonus: You can add them to salads, BYO Bowls (page 215), or Bai's "No Rules" Sandwiches (page 122), or just dip them into Hummus We Love (page 91)!

One 5-pound sack Yukon Gold potatoes

TO BAKE: Preheat the oven to 400°F. Pierce the potatoes' skin before baking to keep them from blowing up inside your oven! Place the potatoes directly on the rack or on a parchment-lined sheet pan. Cook for about 40 minutes or until a fork easily pierces the thickest part of the potato. Turn the oven off and leave the potatoes in the oven until ready to serve. This bakes in some moisture or somehow makes them moist and delicious. If you are not eating the potatoes that day, store them in the fridge.

    TO MICROWAVE: Pierce 2 or 3 potatoes and place them in the microwave. Cook for 8 minutes. Give each potato a squeeze to make sure it feels soft and cooked through. If needed, cook for a few more minutes.

HOW TO COOK KALE

There are as many ways to cook kale as there are to eat it. We like to cook it until it is soft and easy to chew and swallow. Our logic is that if it is easier to eat, we will eat more of it! If you prefer kale blanched or just lightly steamed—great! We like it cooked a lot longer. This is just the way we roll with kale.

SERVES 5–6

2 bunches kale, stems stripped and leaves torn into bite-size pieces

Place the kale in a large pot of boiling water, cover, and cook about 5 minutes, until tender. The trick here is to cook it until it tastes just right for you. Drain in a colander.

    Serve warm alone or with any of our dressings or vinegar.

HOW TO CARAMELIZE ONIONS

These are such a staple in our kitchen! A hot pan is key to caramelizing onions.

MAKES 1½–2 CUPS

1 large onion, diced or julienned—your preference

Place a large pan over high heat—or medium-high heat if you have a nonstick pan (overheating is not good for the pan). When it is hot, add the onions and stir until they start to brown.

Slowly reduce the heat while continuing to stir the onions. Add a teaspoon of water and continue stirring until the onions are browned and cooked through, anywhere from 5 to 15 minutes depending on how you like them, how low your heat is, and how much onion you are cooking.

Serve warm or store covered in the fridge until ready to use.

VARIATION: CARAMELIZED BALSAMIC ONIONS

Add 2 tablespoons balsamic vinegar (see page 95) toward the end of cooking the onions and stir until they are uniformly well coated.

HOW TO COOK ONIONS, GARLIC, AND MUSHROOMS

A nonstick pan is your friend here. Other pans may work, but you may need to add water if the pan gets too dry or the onions start to stick.

MAKES 1½–2 CUPS

1 large onion, diced or julienned—your preference

2 cloves garlic, minced

4 ounces mushrooms, sliced

Place a large nonstick pan over medium-high heat. Add the onions and stir until they become translucent. Slowly reduce the heat to medium and continue stirring to keep the onions from browning. Cook the onions until they are cooked to your liking. Add the garlic once the onions are translucent and softened. Continue stirring until fragrant and done to your liking.

Add the mushrooms to the pan and continue stirring until the mushrooms cook down to your liking. Mushrooms lose quite a bit of fluid as they cook and get fragrant.

Serve warm or store covered in the fridge until ready to use.

TIP:

Mushrooms cook beautifully alone. Sometimes we make an enormous pan of cooked mushrooms for lunch!

CHAPTER 4

POWERFUL
BREAKFASTS

How do you start your day? Do you need to have your breakfast on the go? We have a delicious, pocket-size morning meal in this chapter, Siri's Breakfast Pucks (page 69). Are you a commuter? We have Morning Commute Oats (page 56) or Blueberry Summer Corn Muffins (page 61) for your ride to work.

Are you looking for flavor and fun in the morning? Try our Apple Flax Flapjacks (page 67), Pan-Toasted Pepita Granola (page 55), or Lemon Oatmeal (page 65).

Perhaps you prefer a savory meal with the morning news and you have a little more time to cook? You will dig Ann's Warrior Oats (page 59) or Grits and Greens (page 71).

If you feel morning is the time to get adventurous and swing from a new limb, we suggest Sweet Potato Start (page 72) or Om Oats (page 57).

No matter how you start your day, we hope you will find some way to get plants into your routine, you Plant-Based Woman Warrior, you. Or take a tip from Ann, who insists on finding a way to eat oats in some way to start each day!

PAN-TOASTED PEPITA GRANOLA

To make heart disease-friendly: Do not add walnuts

MAKES ABOUT 2 CUPS

1 cup old-fashioned rolled oats

¼ cup chopped walnuts

¼ cup raw pepitas (pumpkin seeds)

2 tablespoons chia seeds

2 tablespoons flaxseed meal

1 teaspoon cinnamon

3 tablespoons maple syrup

¼ cup raisins or currants, optional

This quick, clever granola recipe fills the kitchen with such an enticing aroma it will wake sleeping teens! My daughters introduced us to this way of making granola after learning it from plant-based YouTuber Maddie Lymburner. Many thanks to Maddie—we can't get enough of sprinkling this on top of oatmeal or just eating it by the handful! This recipe is a joy because it is simple and fun to mix up the flavors (see variations).

1. Place a large pan over medium heat and add the oats. Stir them around while they get a bit fragrant. Add the walnuts and pepitas, stirring until all the ingredients get slightly toasted, 3 to 5 minutes, depending on the size of your pan. Reduce the heat to low and add the chia seeds, flaxseed meal, and cinnamon. Stir for another minute, or until fragrant.

2. Here is the transforming step—add the maple syrup and continue to stir, coating all the ingredients. The syrup will sizzle a bit, which scared us the first time (and the second time). Remove from the heat. Once it has cooled, add the raisins (if using). Store any extra granola in an airtight container within arm's reach, as this will be a favorite!

VARIATIONS:

Once the granola has cooled, try adding hazelnuts (lightly crushed with the bottom of a jar), dried cherries, cashew pieces, nondairy chocolate chips, or dried cranberries. Or stir ½ teaspoon almond extract or vanilla extract into the maple syrup before you add it to the pan.

MORNING COMMUTE OATS

To make heart disease-friendly: Do not add walnuts

SERVES 1-2

½–¾ cup old-fashioned rolled oats

¼ cup fresh or thawed frozen blueberries

1 fresh peach, sliced, or 1 cup canned peach slices, drained

½ banana, sliced

2 teaspoons hemp seeds, optional

1 tablespoon chia seeds

1 tablespoon flaxseed meal

1–2 tablespoons walnuts

1–2 tablespoons almond milk or oat milk, optional

¼ teaspoon cinnamon

Breakfast advice for fellow commuters on eating your oats each morning: Be careful if you place your oatmeal bowl on the roof of your car while you are getting out your keys or packing your car with backpacks or a gym bag—the bowl may fall and spill, and the crows will get to eat your breakfast. Believe me, I have some experience with this! The good news for time-crunched mornings is that this breakfast can be eaten cold and raw! As you head out the door, just pour extra oat milk over the oats, like you do with cold cereal.

Place the oats in a microwaveable bowl. Add just enough water to cover the oats (about 1 cup). Microwave for 1 minute, and then stir a few times. Heat for an additional minute. Repeat for a third minute if needed. Be careful if you do two minutes in a row—the oatmeal might overflow and your bowl will be too hot to hold. Remove the bowl from the microwave and add the blueberries, peaches, banana, hemp seeds (if using), chia seeds, flaxseed meal, walnuts, almond milk (if using), and cinnamon. Commute safely as you breakfast en route to work.

OM OATS

Heart disease-friendly

SERVES 2

½ cup steel-cut oats

½–1 teaspoon minced fresh ginger

¼ cup nutritional yeast

¼ teaspoon minced green finger pepper

¼ teaspoon turmeric

¼ teaspoon coriander

½ teaspoon garam masala

1 tablespoon flaxseed meal

½ cup green peas (frozen is fine), optional

1 cup kale leaves, chopped into strips

¼ cup coarsely chopped cilantro, for garnish, optional

¼ cup fresh pomegranate seeds, for garnish, optional (see note, page 152)

I had my first taste of savory oatmeal decades ago at a meditation retreat. The subtle but delicious flavors are still with me today—hints of lemon, garam masala, ginger, and millet. It was mind opening at the time, perhaps more so than my meditation attempts. I have not been able to exactly recreate it, but this recipe comes quite close to what I recall.

In a medium pot over medium-high heat, stir together the oats with 2¼ cups water, the ginger, nutritional yeast, green pepper, turmeric, coriander, garam masala, flaxseed meal, peas (if using), and kale. Bring to a boil, then reduce to low and simmer for around 20 minutes, or until the oats are cooked and creamy or reach a consistency of your liking, adding more water if needed. Serve garnished with the cilantro and pomegranate seeds (if using).

ANN'S WARRIOR OATS

Heart disease–friendly

**SERVES 2
(OR 1 IF ANN
IS AROUND)**

½ cup steel-cut oats

½ cup shiitake mushrooms, sliced (fresh, frozen, or dried and reconstituted)

2 cups chopped kale, collard greens, Swiss chard, spinach, bok choy, carrot tops, or radish greens (or any combination of greens)

2 tablespoons nutritional yeast

¼–½ teaspoon turmeric

1 teaspoon sriracha or hot sauce of choice, optional

1 tablespoon flaxseed meal

1 tablespoon chia seeds

Ann says she wants to live long and die fast. But good luck finding her stationary long enough to talk about this theory! She does not sit still. Her morning dose of rocket fuel will have you on the go, and also have you "going" regularly! After trying many different routines, this is the breakfast she looks forward to eating every day. She says, "I know I am getting so much power in one fabulous bowl. This is a breakfast I am willing to wake up early to make even when we have to catch a 6:00 a.m. plane!"

1. In a small pot, stir together the oats with 2¼ cups water, the mushrooms, kale, nutritional yeast, turmeric, and sriracha (if using). Heat over medium-high until the mixture starts to boil, but watch carefully because it boils over quickly. Reduce the heat to a simmer, stir, and cook about 10 minutes, or until the mixture begins to thicken a little but is still quite soupy. Ann removes it from the heat at this point, insisting the oats continue to thicken as the dish cools. If you prefer your oats thicker and softer, continue cooking for a couple more minutes.

2. Before serving, add the flaxseed meal and chia seeds for an omega-3 boost.

VARIATIONS:
POLLY'S POWERED-UP WARRIOR OATS

My sister-in-law Polly knows how to power up when it comes to just about anything. After cooking Ann's Warrior Oats, Polly adds:

1 cup fresh greens in the bottom of her big bowl

A sprinkle of nigella seeds/black cumin

A sprinkle of dulse/seaweed flakes

¼ cup fresh microgreens on top of it all (she loves radish)

JANE'S RIS-*OAT*-TO WARRIOR OATS

This variation is an oat-based risotto. After cooking Ann's Warrior Oats for 18 minutes (instead of 10), I add:

¼ cup pickled ginger, for garnish

Black pepper, to taste

BLUEBERRY SUMMER CORN MUFFINS

Heart disease–friendly

MAKES 12 MUFFINS

2 heaping tablespoons chia seeds or flaxseed meal

¾ cup oat flour (see notes)

½ cup cornmeal

½ cup corn flour (see notes)

1 teaspoon baking soda

½ teaspoon baking powder

Pinch of salt, optional

1½ cups corn, fresh off the cob or frozen

½ cup nondairy milk

½ cup applesauce

3 tablespoons maple syrup

2 cups blueberries (see notes)

Add these muffins to your morning and you'll defy hunger all day! Our friend Beth, who is a muffin-making maven, sent us this spot-on recipe. It's also the perfect midday snack to tide you over until dinner.

1. Preheat the oven to 375°F.

2. In a medium bowl, combine the chia seeds with 1 cup water and set aside for 15 minutes.

3. In a large bowl, mix the oat flour, cornmeal, corn flour, baking soda, baking powder, and salt (if using). In the chia seed mixture bowl, stir together the corn, nondairy milk, applesauce, and maple syrup. Pour the wet ingredients into the dry ingredients and mix thoroughly, then fold in the blueberries.

4. Spoon the batter into a nonstick muffin pan using roughly ½ cup batter per muffin well. Bake for 20 to 22 minutes, until golden and firm to touch. Let cool for a few minutes, then release from the pan.

NOTES:

*If you cannot find oat or corn flour or you prefer to make it at home, it's easy to make yourself. Simply blend 1 cup oats in a high-speed blender to make ¾ cup oat flour, or ½ cup cornmeal in a high-speed blender to use as corn flour.

*If you prefer no berries, increase the amount of corn to 2 cups.

BREAKFAST BANANA MUFFINS *or* BREAD

To make heart disease-friendly: Do not add walnuts

MAKES 12 MUFFINS OR 1 LOAF

2 cups oat flour or any flour of choice

½ teaspoon baking soda

1 teaspoon baking powder

1 teaspoon cinnamon

3 ripe medium bananas

½ cup applesauce

¼ cup maple syrup

2 tablespoons flaxseed meal

½ cup raisins

½ cup chopped walnuts, optional

1 tablespoon lemon juice

⅔ cup oat milk or nondairy milk of choice

This recipe was one of our favorites from *Prevent and Reverse Heart Disease*. We've now updated it and we love it all over again! The best part is that it is quick to put together. Be sure to cook it long enough, especially if you are using all oat flour. This is good both hot out of the oven and cold the next day, but it is unbelievably good toasted! It also works with frozen bananas that have been thawed.

1. Preheat the oven to 375°F. Use a nonstick muffin pan or line an 8½ × 4½-inch loaf pan with parchment paper.

2. In a medium bowl, mix together the flour, baking soda, baking powder, and cinnamon.

3. In a separate bowl, mash the bananas with a fork or potato masher. Add the applesauce, maple syrup, flaxseed meal, raisins, walnuts (if using), lemon juice, and oat milk and stir.

4. Add the wet ingredients to the dry ingredients and stir gently until combined. Scoop or pour the batter into the muffin wells or loaf pan. If you are making muffins, bake for 25 to 28 minutes; for bread, bake for 60 to 70 minutes, until browned on the outside and firm yet giving to touch.

LEMON OATMEAL

To make heart disease-friendly: Do not add walnuts

SERVES 1-2

½ cup steel-cut oats

1 teaspoon lemon zest (from about 1 lemon), reserve a pinch for garnish

2–3 tablespoons lemon juice

2–3 tablespoons maple syrup

⅓ cup or more fresh berries of your choice

1 teaspoon chia seeds or flaxseed meal

¼ cup walnuts, toasted, optional

Morning, sunshine! Guess who inspired this recipe? Ann, the lemon-loving Acid Queen herself! Knock your own socks off with this bowl of bright energy. The lemon and maple syrup create a beautiful balance of tart and sweet—a delicious foundation for the fresh berries and toasted walnut toppings. This recipe was the inspiration for our delicious Lemon Pie Squares (page 289). Feel free to adjust the lemon juice and maple syrup to suit your taste.

In a small pot over high heat, stir together the oats with 1½ cups water, the lemon zest, lemon juice, and maple syrup. Bring to a boil, then reduce the heat. Simmer, stirring occasionally, until the oats are cooked to your liking, adding more water if needed. We like our oats to be a bit chewy but personal preferences vary—especially between my mom and me. For this dish, we cook the oats for around 15 minutes, a bit longer than Ann usually likes. Serve topped with the berries, chia seeds, and toasted walnuts (if using).

APPLE FLAX FLAPJACKS

Heart disease–friendly

MAKES ABOUT 12

1 tablespoon flaxseed meal

½ cup oat flour or whole wheat flour (or any combo of the two)

2 tablespoons old-fashioned rolled oats

¼ teaspoon baking powder

½ teaspoon cinnamon

½ cup nondairy milk

1 tablespoon apple cider vinegar

½ teaspoon vanilla

1 apple, cored and sliced into ¼-inch to ⅛-inch thin discs (so thin you can see through them; they will look like flat donut rings!)

Growing up, I devoured stacks of whole wheat pancakes any morning—a gene I passed on to my children. My daughter Crile introduced us to this Apple Flax Flapjacks recipe, which coats apple rings in the batter. These are good plain or with any toppings you can imagine: fresh berries, applesauce, maple syrup, orange zest, sliced bananas, peanut butter, dried cherries, or chia seeds. Or go for it and try them all!

They are a fun, new spin on a classic.

1. In a large bowl, combine the flaxseed meal, flour, oats, baking powder, and cinnamon. Add the nondairy milk, vinegar, and vanilla and stir a few times until just combined.

2. The batter will thicken while you make your flapjacks. Add 2 to 4 tablespoons water, as needed, when the batter needs thinning.

3. Heat a nonstick pan over medium (or medium-low) heat.

4. Submerge an apple ring into the pancake batter—flip and dip as needed to get all sides coated. Place the coated apple ring onto the pan and cook it like a regular pancake. Once the underside is lightly browned, flip and cook the other side for 1 minute, or until browned. Keep a close eye on them, as the thin layer of batter cooks quickly.

SIRI'S BREAKFAST PUCKS

MAKES ABOUT 12

2 cups old-fashioned rolled oats

1 cup peanut butter or almond butter

¼ cup maple syrup

⅓ cup apple butter or pear butter

1 ripe banana, mashed, or ¼ cup water

½ cup raw pepitas (pumpkin seeds)

¼ cup raw sunflower seeds

¼ cup chopped walnuts

¼ cup flaxseed meal

2 tablespoons chia seeds

1 teaspoon cinnamon

¼ teaspoon salt, optional

½ cup raisins, dried cherries, or dried cranberries; chopped dried apricots, dates, figs, or candied ginger; or nondairy chocolate chips

Our neighbor Siri has that rare epicurean gene—everything she makes is delicious. While we were hiking with her one day, she described her breakfast cookie, and it made us crazy hungry, like stomach-growling-we-have-to-make-this-now hungry. And the real thing is just as we imagined—hearty, portable, and filling. We will be hiking with a couple of these in our pockets next time!

1. Preheat the oven to 325°F. Line a sheet pan with parchment paper.

2. In a large bowl, combine the oats, peanut butter, maple syrup, apple butter, banana, pepitas, sunflower seeds, walnuts, flaxseed meal, chia seeds, cinnamon, salt (if using), and dried fruit. If needed, get your hands in there to help mix it.

3. When the batter holds together, scoop it with an ice cream scoop onto the prepared pan. Press down into a puck shape about ⅓ inch thick. The cookies don't spread out while baking, so they can be placed close together.

4. Bake for 16 to 18 minutes, until the edges are browned and a bit crispy. Enjoy immediately or store the cooled cookies in an airtight container. They freeze well, too.

VARIATIONS:

You can make these cookies into different sizes and shapes. For smaller pucks, roll the batter into balls and press down a wee bit so they don't roll around the pan. To make bars, press all the batter flat into the pan before baking, making sure it is level so it cooks evenly. Slice into bars while still warm so they will be easy to separate once they cool.

GRITS and GREENS

Heart disease–friendly

SERVES 2–3

2 cups water or vegetable broth

2 cups unsweetened nondairy milk

1½ cups yellow grits or polenta

1–2 teaspoons onion powder

1–2 teaspoons garlic powder

½ teaspoon turmeric

Pinch of salt, optional

Pinch of ground black pepper

1 bunch your favorite greens (like kale or collard greens)

OPTIONAL TOPPINGS

Hot sauce

Nutritional yeast

Salsa

A wonderful friend of mine, Travis, credits her upbringing in the South with her cool name and her love for grits. Travis says this recipe is her attempt to quantify that which cannot be quantified . . . the creamy, delicious goodness of this southern staple!

Originally, Travis's grits were made with cheese and cream and goodness knows what else. But today, this much lighter version is her favorite way to start her day as a Plant-Based Woman Warrior! We like to use curly kale in this dish, but we also sometimes make it with lacinato kale or collard greens.

1. Make the grits: In a large, heavy-bottomed pot over medium-high heat, bring the broth and nondairy milk to a boil. Add the grits in gradually while stirring constantly. Lower the heat to a simmer and cover. Stir every few minutes to prevent the grits from sticking, adding more liquid (water or broth) if needed. (I usually add ½ to 1 cup water while cooking.) Add the onion powder, garlic powder, and turmeric. Cook for 20 to 25 minutes, until tender to your liking. Remove from the heat and season with salt (if using) and pepper. Be sure to taste the grits so you can adjust the seasoning if need be, and love them the way we do!

2. Make the greens: Strip the spines off your greens and chop or tear the leaves into big, bite-size pieces. Bring a large pot of water to a boil and cook the greens for about 5 minutes (or steam in a pot with a steamer basket), or until tender and bright green.

3. To assemble, place the grits in a bowl and top with the greens. (Or experiment! Mix them up together, or place the greens on the bottom and the grits on top, or place them side by side, or use separate plates.) Top with hot sauce, nutritional yeast, or salsa—whatever helps you jump-start your day.

SWEET POTATO START

To make heart disease-friendly: Do not add peanut butter or peanuts

SERVES 2

1 sweet potato, cooked (see page 48)

2 tablespoons peanut butter, or more as needed

Lime juice, to taste

1 tablespoon coarsely chopped peanuts, for garnish

A friend told me her favorite weekly meeting at work always begins with a discussion about breakfast. One of her coworkers recently revealed she likes to start the day by eating half a sweet potato with a thin layer of peanut butter and a squeeze of lime. Brilliant! Try holding this morning treat in your hand like a hot dog and eat the skin and all!

Keeping the skin intact, slice the cooked sweet potato in half lengthwise. Spread the peanut butter on the flesh side of the sweet potato. Squeeze the lime juice over the peanut butter to your liking—some people hesitate to add lime, but it is a game changer. Garnish with the coarsely chopped peanuts for texture.

OPEN-FACED CHICKPEA OMELET 3.0

Heart disease–friendly

MAKES 2

1 cup diced onion

1 cup diced mushrooms

2 cups packed spinach

1 cup chickpea flour

1 teaspoon flaxseed meal

½ teaspoon onion powder

½ teaspoon garlic powder

¼ teaspoon white pepper

¼ teaspoon ground black pepper

¼ teaspoon turmeric

⅓ cup nutritional yeast

½ teaspoon baking soda

OPTIONAL TOPPINGS

1 tomato, diced

Salsa

Hot sauce

Dulse/seaweed flakes

This breakfast option reinvents itself all the time. We love it smothered in vegetables and salsa—just a beautiful sight—or with crumbled Bacon Tempeh (page 113). Add whatever you like to your omelet. If you are into having omelets for dinner, serve with a Warrior Salad (see chapter 7). Oh, one more mind-blowing suggestion, try this with Mommy's Mushroom Gravy 3.0 (page 87).

1. In a pan over medium-high heat, cook the onions while stirring constantly as they brown. Slowly turn the heat down to medium (add a tablespoon of water if the pan gets dry). Add the mushrooms to the pan. Continue to stir for 3 to 5 more minutes, until the mushrooms are cooked through. Add the spinach and continue to stir until the leaves wilt. Set aside and keep warm, if possible.

2. In a small bowl, combine the chickpea flour, flaxseed meal, onion powder, garlic powder, white pepper, black pepper, turmeric, nutritional yeast, and baking soda. Add 1½ cups water and stir until the batter is smooth.

3. In a large, nonstick pan over medium heat, pour the batter as if you are making an 8- to 9-inch-wide pancake. When the underside is browned, after about a minute or two, flip the omelet like a pancake. After another minute or so, check to see if the bottom side is cooked to your liking. When ready, transfer the omelet to a plate with a large spatula. Repeat to make the other omelet.

4. Load half of each omelet with the reserved cooked vegetables and fold the other half of the omelet over like a taco. Add toppings, if desired, and enjoy!

PESTO

LEMON Tahini

Cilantro-Mint

same Ginger

Teriyaki

Original Marinara

SPICY Almond

Limet Sweet Corn

WALNUT GINGER

THAI PEA

GREEN GODDE

CHAPTER 5

SECRET WEAPONS:
SAUCES, HUMMUS, DRESSINGS, SALSAS, and a GUACAMOLE

There is no other way to put it. This section contains our secret weapons—the flavor bombs that make all the difference. These essentials add a savory zing to our dishes and zesty complement to each bite. Dive into this section and come out swinging!

WALNUT GINGER SAUCE and DRESSING

MAKES ABOUT 1½ CUPS

1 cup walnut pieces

1 clove garlic

2 tablespoons low-sodium tamari

2 tablespoons rice vinegar

2 tablespoons minced fresh ginger

1 tablespoon maple syrup, optional

1 squirt hot sauce, your choice

This sauce grabs us with its creamy, sharp flavor and bite—it makes us want to bite back! We adore this on any Build Your Own Bowl, especially the Buddha Bowl (page 221). This is a twist on our classic walnut sauce—a foundational sauce we have loved for decades.

In a food processor or high-speed blender, place the walnuts, garlic, tamari, rice vinegar, ginger, maple syrup (if using), hot sauce, and ⅓ cup water and blend until smooth.

TERIYAKI SAUCE

Heart disease–friendly

MAKES 1 CUP

½ cup low-sodium tamari

¼ cup maple syrup

3 tablespoons ketchup or tomato paste

1 tablespoon minced fresh ginger

¼ cup toasted sesame seeds

If someone were to ask us what our family's favorite sauce is, this one would be the knee-jerk answer for just about everyone. Try baking this on tofu or tempeh (see the Teriyaki Tofu or Tempeh Cubes, page 169). Or use this flavored weaponry drizzled over the BYO Forbidden Bowl (page 219), Balanced Rice Noodle Bowl (page 227), or any bowl, salad, grains, or greens of your choice.

In a small bowl, combine the tamari, maple syrup, ketchup, ginger, and sesame seeds. Use as is or, if you'd like a thicker sauce, transfer to a food processor or high-speed blender and blend until it reaches your desired consistency. The sesame seeds will make the sauce thicker.

THAI PEANUT SAUCE

To make heart disease–friendly: Use the Low-Fat Peanut Sauce variation below

MAKES ABOUT 1½ CUPS

½ cup peanut butter

2 teaspoons minced fresh ginger

2 tablespoons low-sodium tamari

2 tablespoons maple syrup

1 tablespoon rice vinegar

2 tablespoons lime juice

¼ teaspoon red pepper flakes

Divine. We have always felt this way about peanut sauce. We double the recipe each time we prepare it. Add this transformative sauce to your BYO Balanced Rice Noodle Bowl (page 227) or Roots and Shoots Bowl (page 223) and your dinner will be a winner.

In a high-speed blender, place the peanut butter, ginger, tamari, maple syrup, rice vinegar, lime juice, pepper flakes, and ½ cup water and blend. Continue adding water, up to ⅓ cup more, until it reaches your desired consistency.

VARIATION: LOW-FAT PEANUT SAUCE

Make a low-fat peanut sauce with a peanut butter substitute like PB2 Pure Peanut Powder or Crazy Richard's 100% Pure Peanut Powder (available in some stores or on Amazon). Neither product has added sugar or salt, and both have reduced fat.

3 tablespoons oil-free, no-tahini hummus

3 tablespoons peanut butter powder

2 tablespoons brown rice vinegar

1 teaspoon minced fresh ginger

1 tablespoon white balsamic vinegar (see page 95) or 2 teaspoons maple syrup

¼ teaspoon red pepper flakes

In a small bowl, mix together the hummus, peanut butter powder, 2 tablespoons water, brown rice vinegar, ginger, balsamic vinegar, and red pepper flakes and stir until well combined and smooth. Add an additional teaspoon or more of water, if needed, to reach desired consistency.

SPICY ALMOND SAUCE

MAKES ABOUT 1½ CUPS

⅔ cup almond butter

1 tablespoon white miso

1 tablespoon low-sodium tamari

2 cloves garlic

2 dates, pitted (we prefer Medjool)

1 tablespoon hot sauce (we prefer sriracha)

1 teaspoon minced serrano or jalapeño pepper

In our households, peanut sauce reigns supreme as the topping of choice for veggies, rice, noodles, and bowls. But I am sensing the beginnings of a coup—this Spicy Almond Sauce may be close to taking the throne! Enjoy this sauce on a BYO Balanced Rice Noodle Bowl (page 227) or over rice and Sesame Ginger–Topped Tofu or Tempeh (page 171). It's also delicious on rice noodles, atop veggies, or on a BYO Buddha Bowl bar (page 221).

In a food processor or high-speed blender, place the almond butter, miso, tamari, garlic, dates, hot sauce, pepper, and 1 cup water and blend until smooth. Use right away or seal and store in a sealed container in the fridge until ready for use.

TANGY LIME and SWEET CORN SAUCE

Heart disease–friendly

MAKES ABOUT 2 CUPS

3 ears uncooked fresh corn (preferred) or one 16-ounce package thawed frozen corn

1 small sweet onion (about ⅓–½ cup chopped)

½ cup low-sodium vegetable broth

1 clove garlic, chopped

Zest of 1 lime

2 tablespoons lime juice

2 tablespoons lemon white balsamic vinegar or any white balsamic vinegar (see page 95)

The following comment from one of our recipe testers nails it: "OMG!! I was a little suspicious about this recipe, but WOW, this is AWESOME sauce!" My parents first discovered a basic sauce made with corn at a restaurant called Casa de Luz in Austin, Texas, while visiting my older brother Rip. At home we figured out how to make it ourselves, and we have added our own twists over the years, but it is just as delicious as the day we first tasted it. The first three ingredients alone—corn, onion, and vegetable broth—make an easy, fabulous sauce on greens, beans, or anything that needs a lift. Adding the garlic, along with a hit of bright lime and vinegar, takes it to an all-new level. We particularly love this served over brown rice or quinoa, then topped with black beans, cherry tomatoes, more corn(!), a dash of chili powder, and fresh cilantro.

Cut the corn off the cobs and scrape the cobs to extract any small pieces or fluid. Place the fresh corn and fluid (or thawed frozen corn, if using), onion, and vegetable broth in a high-speed blender and blend until smooth, scraping down the sides. Put the mixture in a pan and cook it like scrambled eggs, until it just begins to bubble a little. You can use the sauce as is after this step, or add the garlic, lime zest, lime juice, and balsamic vinegar and stir until fully heated. If the sauce is too thick, add more vegetable broth. This sauce is best served hot over anything!

SESAME GINGER SAUCE

Heart disease–friendly

MAKES ABOUT 2 CUPS

⅔ cup sesame seeds

3 tablespoons low-sodium tamari, plus more as needed to taste

3 tablespoons maple syrup

3 tablespoons minced fresh ginger, plus more as needed to taste

Squirt of hot sauce, your favorite

Just the name of this sauce makes us hungry. Anything with ginger and anything with sesame speaks our love language; we pour this on our BYO Forbidden Bowl (page 219) and Roots and Shoots Bowl (page 223).

In a small pan over medium heat, toast the sesame seeds until lightly browned and fragrant. Remove from the heat and pour into a high-speed blender or food processor. Blend until the sesame seeds start to break open and stick to the sides. Add the tamari, maple syrup, ginger, and up to 1 cup water (or enough to reach your desired consistency) and blend for 2 to 3 minutes, until smooth. Add the squirt of hot sauce and blend again. Taste and add more tamari or ginger if desired.

GREEN GODDESS SAUCE and DRESSING

To make heart disease-friendly: Substitute 15 ounces drained and rinsed cannellini beans for the cashews

MAKES ABOUT 1¾ CUPS

¾ cup cashews, soaked (see note)

½ cup tightly packed parsley leaves and stems

½ cup tightly packed cilantro leaves and stems

½ cup tightly packed basil leaves and stems

3 tablespoons lime juice

2 tablespoons apple cider vinegar

1 tablespoon maple syrup

¼ teaspoon salt, optional

Dress your greens with greens! This Green Goddess Sauce adds a wonderful cooling and balanced flavor to anything. Try it as a layer in a sandwich, with BYO Bowls, atop a salad, alone with brown rice, or as a dip. We like to use it dolloped on Brian's Red Bean Chili (page 251), on the BYO Buddha Bowl (page 221), or as a tasty dip for Cauliflower Fritters (page 181). We often double this recipe. If you end up loving it as much as we do, you can also add a wee bit more water and use it as a salad dressing.

Drain the cashews. In a food processor or high-speed blender, place the cashews, parsley, cilantro, basil, lime juice, vinegar, maple syrup, salt (if using), and ¾ cup water and blend. Add an extra tablespoon of water if you prefer a thinner consistency.

NOTE:

Soak the cashews in warm water until they expand a bit, about 1 hour.

VARIATION: HOT GREEN GODDESS DRESSING

Our young and daring videographers dig this gentle dressing, but they prefer a hot kick to the palate—so they squirt and swirl in sriracha to make a delicious Hot Green Goddess Dressing.

LEMON TAHINI SAUCE

MAKES ABOUT 1½ CUPS

½ cup tahini

½ cup warm water, more or less for desired consistency

¼ cup lemon juice

¼ cup rice vinegar

2 tablespoons maple syrup

Oh, does this sauce have you covered. It is the definition of mellow and agreeable. If you are a ginger lover, try adding grated or minced ginger to the mix! Baked potatoes and corn on the cob scream for a hit of Lemon Tahini Sauce. Try it on the BYO Braw Barley Bowl (page 231), too, or Buddha Bowl (page 221). You can even eat it on toast!

In a food processor or high-speed blender, place the tahini, water, lemon juice, rice vinegar, and maple syrup. Blend until smooth and serve.

CILANTRO-MINT SAUCE

MAKES ABOUT 1½ CUPS

½ cup mint leaves

½ cup cilantro leaves and stems

¾ cup almond milk or
oat milk, more or less
for desired consistency

⅓ cup cashews, soaked
(see note)

1 teaspoon cumin seeds

2 teaspoons minced fresh
ginger

⅛ teaspoon minced green
finger pepper

2 tablespoons lime juice

Pinch of salt, optional

This cooling sauce goes deliciously with our Cauliflower Fritters (page 181) or other spicy dishes. It meant the world to me when our pal Koyen, who grew up on Indian food, flipped over this sauce—she called it real chutney! Oh, I swooned hearing that compliment.

In a food processor or high-speed blender, blend the mint and cilantro until a green pulp forms. Add the almond milk and blend until combined. Drain the cashews and add to the blender along with the cumin seeds, ginger, finger pepper, lime juice, and salt (if using), and blend until the sauce is smooth, green, and beautiful.

NOTE:

Soak the cashews in warm water until they expand a bit, about 1 hour.

ORIGINAL
MARINARA

Heart disease-friendly

MAKES 6+ CUPS

1 cup finely chopped onion

1–2 cloves garlic, minced

1 tablespoon dried oregano

1 teaspoon dried thyme

1 tablespoon chopped
fresh basil

26 ounces strained tomatoes
(see note)

26 ounces finely chopped
tomatoes (see note)

2 tablespoons maple syrup
or 1–2 large, well-mashed
or pureed Medjool dates

½ teaspoon salt, optional

Marinara gets its name from the Italian sailors, or *marina*, whose sea trade brought goods from all around the world home to Italy. Tomatoes, garlic, olive oil, and dried herbs would not spoil on long journeys, so when sailors found themselves stuck at sea for months at a time, these ingredients would come together to create marinara sauce. The same ingredients are the basis of marinara today. Ahoy—here is a healthy version of marinara that we land lovers can enjoy!

1. In a large pan over medium-high heat, cook the onion for a minute or two. Add the garlic and cook for another minute or two, until the onion softens and browns slightly and the garlic is fragrant. If the pan bottom gets dry, add a teaspoon of water as needed. Reduce the heat to medium-low and add the oregano, thyme, and basil. Stir until the onion and garlic are well coated with the herbs.

2. Add the strained tomatoes, chopped tomatoes, maple syrup, and salt (if using) and stir over low heat. Continue to simmer the sauce to your desired thickness—we all have different consistency preferences. We usually cook it between 8 and 15 minutes. Your call.

NOTE:

We love the Pomì brand of boxed strained and chopped tomatoes.

BOYFRIEND BOLOGNESE SAUCE

Heart disease–friendly

MAKES 5+ CUPS

½ cup diced onion

2 cloves garlic, minced

6 ounces tempeh, crumbled

4 ounces white mushrooms, diced

1 tablespoon low-sodium tamari

¼ teaspoon fennel seeds, optional

½ teaspoon red pepper flakes

1 tablespoon maple syrup

3 cups Original Marinara (page 84)

Fresh oregano, for garnish

The aroma from the kitchen had our stomachs growling. It was my daughter's night to cook dinner with her boyfriend, and when they presented the feast on the table, we knew it was worth the wait. When we asked, "What is this gorgeous, hearty red sauce?," Ben proudly replied, "It's Boyfriend Bolognese Sauce." We loved the name and the way this recipe creatively adds mushrooms and tempeh to our Original Marinara (opposite) sauce. The fennel seeds are optional, but we enjoy the layer of taste they add. This sauce has tons of deep flavor. It's a keeper—let's hope the boyfriend is, too!

In a large pan over high heat, cook the onions until they soften and become slightly browned and fragrant. If the pan bottom gets dry, add a teaspoon of water as needed. Reduce the heat to medium-high and add the garlic, tempeh, and mushrooms. Cook for about 3 minutes, or until the mushrooms shrink and the tempeh is warm throughout. Reduce the heat to medium-low and add the tamari, fennel seeds, red pepper flakes, maple syrup, and marinara. Cook for 5 to 8 minutes, until the sauce is thick and well combined (it is a thicker, heartier sauce than other pasta sauces). When serving, garnish with oregano.

MOMMY'S MUSHROOM GRAVY 3.0

Heart disease–friendly

MAKES ABOUT 3 CUPS

1 large sweet onion, chopped

3 cloves garlic, minced

16 ounces mushrooms, sliced

2 cups vegetable broth

2 teaspoons white miso

2 tablespoons low-sodium tamari

2 tablespoons oat flour or whole wheat flour, optional

Ground black pepper, to taste

We *love* this recipe so much. And since it has changed in small, nuanced ways over the years, we continue to refine it in our cookbooks. This recipe uses more onion, more mushrooms, and no alcohol. The flour is also optional as I often accidentally forget to add it and it still turns out delish (though Ann proclaims the flour is a *must!*).

1. In a medium pan over medium-high heat, cook the onion. Allow the onion to brown a little while stirring, adding a splash of water to the pan if it starts to burn. Add the garlic and mushrooms and continue cooking until the mushrooms soften, again adding a little water as needed to keep the mixture from burning.

2. Add 1 cup of the broth to the pan and stir. In a small bowl, place the remaining cup of broth with the miso, tamari, and flour (if using), and stir until the miso has dissolved. Add the broth mixture to the pan. Continue cooking until the gravy thickens to your liking. Season with pepper to taste. Serve warm.

AVOCADO

We love pesto, all kinds of pesto. And we know we are not alone. This is a richer sauce since it has avocado as its foundation. So, it is an occasional treat for all. Basil-based pesto is a tried-and-true favorite, but cilantro or parsley pestos are also out of this world! The smooth texture of the avocado gives this a beautiful silken texture when spread on toast, served with pasta, added to a salad, or enjoyed as a dip.

MAKES ABOUT ⅔ CUP

1 ripe avocado

½ cup tightly packed basil, cilantro, or parsley leaves and stems, roughly chopped

½ clove garlic

1–2 teaspoons lemon juice

Pinch of salt, to taste, optional

In a mini food processor or a small high-speed blender (if you do not have a mini food processor or small blender, consider doubling the recipe so it will fill the basin), place the avocado, basil, garlic, lemon juice, and salt (if using) and blend until roughly combined. Add a splash of water if you want a thinner sauce.

WALNUT

This Walnut Pesto with parsley won the empty bowl contest around our table. Wow, do these two flavors pair well together! Other winning combos are cilantro-walnut or basil-walnut pesto. Try them all!

MAKES ABOUT ⅔ CUP

⅔ cup walnuts, lightly toasted

½ cup tightly packed parsley, cilantro, or basil leaves and stems, roughly chopped

½ clove garlic

1 tablespoon lemon juice

¼ teaspoon salt, optional

In a mini food processor or a small high-speed blender (if you do not have a mini food processor or small blender, consider doubling the recipe so it will fill the basin), place the walnuts, parsley, garlic, lemon juice, salt (if using), and ⅓ cup water and blend, adding more water as needed, until the mixture reaches your desired consistency.

CASHEW PESTO

MAKES ABOUT ⅔ CUP

⅓ cup cashews, soaked (see note)

1 cup tightly packed cilantro, basil, or parsley leaves and stems, roughly chopped

1 clove garlic

1 teaspoon low-sodium tamari, or to taste

1 teaspoon lemon juice

Cashews offer a strong, smooth foundation for this pesto. We adore cilantro—and this pesto. If cilantro is not your thing, try this with basil or parsley instead.

Drain the cashews. In a mini food processor or a small high-speed blender (if you do not have a mini food processor or small blender, consider doubling the recipe so it will fill the basin), place the cashews, cilantro, garlic, tamari, lemon juice, and ¼ cup water. Blend until the mixture is smooth yet flecked with cilantro. Add another ¼ cup of water if desired for consistency.

NOTE:

Soak the cashews in warm water until they expand a bit, about 1 hour.

for **BLACK BEAN HUMMUS**

for **ROASTED GARLIC HUMMUS**

for **BALSAMIC HUMMUS**

HUMMUS WE LOVE

for **LEMON HUMMUS**

for **HICKORY SMOKEHOUSE HUMMUS**

HUMMUS WE LOVE

To make heart disease-friendly: Leave out the tahini

MAKES ABOUT 1¼ CUPS

15 ounces canned low-salt or no-salt chickpeas

2 cloves garlic, or to taste

2 tablespoons lemon juice

1–2 tablespoons low-sodium tamari

2 tablespoons tahini, optional

¼ teaspoon cumin

2 squirts hot sauce, your favorite

¼–½ cup aquafaba, reserved from chickpea can

We love hummus. It is our go-to whenever we need a layer of flavor, moisture, or mortar to hold things together—literally. One of the secrets to this recipe is to reserve and add the water from the chickpea can, otherwise known as aquafaba. We find that aquafaba adds depth and flavor to hummus, and as a bonus, we feel resourceful using up an ingredient that would otherwise be wasted. You can make this recipe with or without the tahini.

In a food processor or high-speed blender, place the chickpeas, garlic, lemon juice, tamari, tahini (if using), cumin, hot sauce, and ¼ cup aquafaba. Blend until well combined and smooth, adding up to ¼ cup more aquafaba until the hummus reaches your desired consistency. Serve or store in a sealed container in the fridge for up to 5 days.

VARIATIONS:
LEMON HUMMUS

Seeking a little more sunshine? A little more pucker and brightness to your day? Try our Lemon Hummus. It is really easy. Add 2 extra tablespoons of lemon juice and the zest of half a lemon to the basic recipe.

BALSAMIC HUMMUS

The key to this variation is to find your favorite infused balsamic vinegar (see page 95). These astounding vinegars are thick, sweet, and packed with flavor. Add 2 tablespoons balsamic vinegar to the basic recipe.

BLACK BEAN HUMMUS

This is a fun change of pace—and so easy! We double the recipe and use 1 can (15 ounces) of black beans and 1 can (15 ounces) of chickpeas and lime instead of lemon. Add a pinch of chipotle powder if that's your thing. When doubling the amount of aquafaba in this recipe, if the aquafaba from the chickpea can is not ½ cup, simply add water.

recipe continues

ROASTED GARLIC HUMMUS

Garlic is a natural antibiotic and helps fight off high blood pressure, inflammation, and vampires. Roasted garlic is our favorite, as it brings out the pirate within—the cloves are like soft culinary gems.

To roast garlic, slice the pointy top off the garlic bulb, remove any extra loose, papery skin, and wrap the bulb in foil with the cut end facing up. Roast for 45 to 60 minutes at 400°F. Remove from the oven and unwrap. Once the bulb is cool enough to handle, gently squeeze each roasted clove from its wrappings.

Add 4 to 6 cloves of roasted garlic to the basic recipe and blend.

HICKORY SMOKEHOUSE HUMMUS

Try this smoky, hickory hummus on your next sandwich. It will make you feel as though you are in front of an open campfire, feasting before you hit the trails for another day in the great North, Badlands, Highlands, or just your own backyard.

Add ½ teaspoon smoked paprika and ¼ teaspoon liquid smoke to the basic recipe and blend.

Romaine Dippers

If you are on the road or just don't have time to make a salad, use romaine hearts to add an easy green to your day! Just twist off the bottom of a romaine heart with your powerful plant-strong hands, arrange the leaves prettily in a bowl, and use them as dippers to eat with chili or hummus or any dip or dish that needs greens. You can't beat that for being easy!

THOUSAND ISLAND HUMMUS

Looking for something reminiscent of a Reuben sandwich or that special sauce in a Big Mac? Try our Thousand Island Hummus as a dip, on a sandwich, or on our Woman Warrior Burgers (page 238).

15 ounces canned low-salt or no-salt chickpeas

2 cloves garlic, or to taste

3 tablespoons lemon juice

1–2 tablespoons low-sodium tamari

2 tablespoons tahini, optional

¼ teaspoon cumin

¼ cup pickle relish, your choice

2 green onions, chopped

2–3 tablespoons ketchup

2–3 squirts hot sauce, your favorite

¼–½ cup aquafaba, reserved from chickpea can

In a food processor, place the chickpeas, garlic, lemon juice, tamari, tahini (if using), cumin, relish, green onions, ketchup, hot sauce, and ¼ cup aquafaba. Blend until well combined and smooth, adding up to ¼ cup more aquafaba until the hummus reaches your desired consistency.

Add to any salad, sandwich, or bowl, or feature as a dip.

ANN *and* ESSY'S FAVORITE DRESSING

IN THE PINK DRESSING

CRILE'S LIGHT LEMON DRESSING

BARITONE DRESSING

STRAWBERRY BALSAMIC DRESSING

3-2-1 HUM DRESSING

LIGHTNING DRESSING

WALNUT HORSERADISH DRESSING

"The Right Vinegar Makes *All* the Difference!"
—Ann

The right vinegar transforms a dressing, a meal, or a dish. When we list balsamic vinegar as an ingredient in our recipes, we are referring to high-quality balsamic vinegar. It is thicker and sweeter and may be infused with flavor. It is hard to believe how palatable and delicious it is until you have tried it. Once you do, you'll agree these high-quality vinegars are worth every penny. We love the vinegars from the Olive Tap, the Olive Scene, and California Balsamic.

ANN and ESSY'S FAVORITE DRESSING

To make heart disease-friendly: Use oil- and tahini-free hummus

MAKES ½ CUP

2 tablespoons Hummus We Love (page 91) or any oil-free hummus

2 tablespoons orange juice or ½ orange, sections and juice

2 tablespoons balsamic vinegar (see page 95)

2 teaspoons mustard, your favorite

1 teaspoon minced fresh ginger

If you were to tap into Ann or Essy with a spile as a Vermonter would into a sugar maple tree, out would course this dressing. They eat this every day. Every single day.

In a small bowl or lidded jar, combine the hummus, orange juice, vinegar, mustard, and ginger. Stir or shake until well combined. Toss with your salad and enjoy.

VARIATION:

For a creamier dressing, add 1 tablespoon nutritional yeast.

BARITONE DRESSING

MAKES ABOUT ¾ CUP

3 tablespoons warm water

2 tablespoons tahini, almond butter, or any nut butter

2 tablespoons white miso

1 large or 2 small cloves garlic, minced

2 tablespoons rice vinegar

1 tablespoon maple syrup

2 teaspoons low-sodium tamari

1–2 teaspoons sriracha or hot sauce of choice, to taste

1 green onion, finely chopped

If this dressing could sing, its tone would be deep and soothing. Dress your salad with it and sway with these delicious tones bite after bite.

In a small bowl or lidded jar, combine the warm water, tahini, and miso. Add the garlic, vinegar, maple syrup, tamari, sriracha, and green onion. Stir or shake until well combined. Serve on salads, greens, or grains, or drizzle on your sandwich!

3-2-1 HUM DRESSING

To make heart disease-friendly: Use oil- and tahini-free hummus

MAKES ½ CUP

3 tablespoons balsamic vinegar (see page 95)

2 tablespoons mustard, your favorite

1 tablespoon maple syrup

2–3 tablespoons Hummus We Love (page 91) or any oil-free hummus

Hands down, one of our favorite dressings is the "3-2-1," a perfect balance of balsamic vinegar, mustard, and maple syrup. This recipe adds a dollop of hummus to stretch it out and give it more body. So easy! All our kids make it with ease: They just need to remember 3-2-1 plus hummus!

In a bowl or lidded jar, combine the vinegar, mustard, maple syrup, and hummus. Stir or shake until well combined.

CRILE'S LIGHT LEMON DRESSING

To make heart disease–friendly: Use oil- and tahini-free hummus

MAKES ½ CUP

3 tablespoons lemon balsamic vinegar (see page 95)

2 tablespoons spicy brown mustard

1 tablespoon lemon juice, or to taste

1 tablespoon Lemon Hummus (page 91) or Hummus We Love (page 91)

1 tablespoon maple syrup

This light and bright dressing, full of lemon love, proves that Crile is clearly Acid Queen Ann's granddaughter. This recipe is a riff on Jane's original 3-2-1 Dressing, the flavor foundation on which Crile was raised. Crile recommends putting this dressing on a leafy salad with accents of toasted nuts and fresh berries, as it adds to the salad's lightness and brightness.

In a small bowl or lidded jar, combine the vinegar, mustard, lemon juice, hummus, and maple syrup. Stir or shake until well combined.

STRAWBERRY BALSAMIC DRESSING

Heart disease–friendly

MAKES ABOUT 1½ CUPS

1 cup sliced fresh or thawed frozen strawberries

¼ cup white balsamic vinegar (see page 95)

¼ cup diced red or white onion

2 teaspoons Dijon mustard

¼ teaspoon ground black pepper

When you need a delicious and beautiful knockout dressing, this is it. And best of all, it is mostly fruit!

In a food processor or high-speed blender, place the strawberries, vinegar, onion, mustard, and pepper and blend until well combined and smooth.

WALNUT HORSERADISH DRESSING

MAKES ABOUT ⅔ CUP

½ cup raw walnut pieces

1–1½ tablespoons prepared horseradish (jarred), to taste

2 teaspoons apple cider vinegar

2 teaspoons maple syrup

1 teaspoon mustard, your choice

Horseradish root offers intense flavor, and a little goes a long way. When Brian first made this, I could not get enough; I ate the whole huge bowl of salad myself! The subtle zing of this dressing is incredible. If it speaks to you like it does to me, I recommend doubling the recipe—I always love having some extra around. This dressing also works as a sandwich spread.

In a food processor or high-speed blender, place the walnuts, horseradish, vinegar, maple syrup, mustard, and ¼ cup water. Blend until well combined. This dressing is slightly thick, similar to a Caesar dressing, but if you like a thinner consistency, add another ¼ cup water.

IN THE PINK

Heart disease–friendly

MAKES ABOUT 1⅓ CUPS

1 medium beet (about 1 cup sliced), cooked and roughly chopped

2 large cloves garlic, roughly chopped

Zest of 1 lemon

2–3 tablespoons lemon juice

1 tablespoon balsamic vinegar, preferably lemon balsamic (see page 95)

4 tablespoons orange juice or ½ orange, peeled

This is a not-so-sneaky way to get all that heart-protective endothelial benefit from beets. And it will make your salad a striking red color! If you are using Chioggia beets, the dressing will be a beautiful pink instead of beet red.

1. In a food processor or high-speed blender, blend the beet and garlic until combined.

2. Scrape the sides of the processor, and add the lemon zest, lemon juice, vinegar, and orange juice and blend until well combined and smooth.

LIGHTNING DRESSING

Heart disease–friendly

MAKES ABOUT 1 CUP

1 clove garlic, minced

2 teaspoons minced fresh ginger

½ jalapeño pepper, seeded and minced

Juice of 1 lime (about 2 tablespoons)

Zest of 1 lime

2 tablespoons rice vinegar

5 tablespoons low-sodium tamari

5 tablespoons maple syrup

3 pinches red pepper flakes

Here it is, lightning in a bottle! We have been struck by this dressing and are forever changed. Seriously, this one tops the list! Over the years we have loved the depth, heat, and flavor of this beautifully balanced Asian dressing. It pairs well with our BYO Forbidden Bowl (page 219) or Balanced Rice Noodle Bowl (page 227).

In a small, lidded container, combine the garlic, ginger, jalapeño, lime juice and zest, rice vinegar, tamari, maple syrup, and red pepper flakes. Seal and shake, shake, shake: That lightning needs to get all fired up. Serve over salad, greens, or grains.

RED RADISH
GRAPE SALSA

VIBRANT
MANGO SALSA

PEACH SALSA

BRIAN'S
FRESH SALSA

WATERMELON
SALSA

PEACH SALSA

Heart disease-friendly

MAKES ABOUT 2 CUPS

1 medium tomato, diced (about 1 cup)

¼ red bell pepper, diced

½–1 jalapeño pepper, minced

¼ medium onion, diced (about ½ cup)

2 peaches, cubed (larger than the diced tomato)

¼ cup roughly chopped cilantro

2 tablespoons lime juice

¼ teaspoon ground black pepper, or to taste

This clever recipe came our way from Mark LaMonda, who attended one of our virtual cooking classes. It exemplifies the breadth of what salsa offers—tones of sweetness, savoriness, and spice, along with a juicy richness. Adjust the amount of jalapeño according to the level of heat you like!

In a medium bowl, combine the tomato, red pepper, jalapeño, onion, peaches, cilantro, lime juice, and black pepper until well mixed. Add more pepper to taste if desired.

BRIAN'S FRESH SALSA

Heart disease–friendly

MAKES ABOUT 2½ CUPS

2 cups cherry tomatoes

1 green bell pepper, chopped

¼ cup tightly packed parsley leaves and stems

2–3 green onions, roughly chopped

2–3 tablespoons lime juice

½ teaspoon chili powder, or to taste

½ teaspoon garlic powder, or to taste

½ teaspoon onion powder, or to taste

Pinch of salt, optional

Brian combines the bounty of summer into a salsa so refreshing we could drink it. He always makes a big batch, and it never lasts more than a day. This is the salsa you build your dinner around. It is ideal to make with cherry tomatoes still warm from the garden!

In a food processor or high-speed blender, place the tomatoes, green pepper, parsley, green onions, lime juice, chili powder, garlic powder, onion powder, and salt (if using). Pulse until well combined but a few visible chunks remain. If you like a smoother salsa, pulse a few more times. We like the way this salsa pours right out of the food processor.

VIBRANT MANGO SALSA

Heart disease–friendly

SERVES 4

1 mango, cubed

½ cucumber, diced including peel

½ red bell pepper, cubed

¼ small sweet onion, chopped

¼ cup coarsely chopped cilantro leaves and stems, optional

2 tablespoons white balsamic vinegar (see page 95)

2 pinches red pepper flakes

This tastes as good as it looks and enhances anything from a plate of rice and beans to just plain rice. It is also delicious on a crisp-baked corn tortilla.

In a small bowl, combine the mango, cucumber, bell pepper, onion, cilantro (if using), vinegar, and red pepper flakes. Allow the mixture to sit for a bit for the flavors to mingle. As tempting as it may be, don't eat it all right away!

WATERMELON SALSA

Heart disease-friendly

MAKES ABOUT 3 CUPS

2 cups diced watermelon

1 cup cherry tomatoes, quartered

½ cup minced sweet onion

⅓ cup coarsely chopped parsley leaves and stems

⅓ cup coarsely chopped cilantro leaves and stems, optional

2–3 tablespoons lime juice, to taste

If the watermelons are good, we consume one a day in the summer: cut into wedges, balls, or squares or eaten right out of the rind with a spoon. Our secret is anointing the gorgeous pink fruit with lime! It is a sublime balance of sweet and pucker. This salsa grew out of our love for these astounding summer flavors. It elevates quinoa, white and sweet potatoes, rice, greens, and beans. Or just eat it on its own!

In a medium bowl, place the watermelon, tomatoes, onion, parsley, cilantro (if using), and 2 tablespoons lime juice. Mix until the ingredients are well coated with the lime juice. Taste and add more lime juice if needed.

RED RADISH GRAPE SALSA

Heart disease-friendly

MAKES ABOUT 2 CUPS

½ cup finely chopped radishes

½ cup quartered cherry tomatoes

½ cup quartered red grapes

½ cup thinly sliced green onions

¼ cup parsley, coarsely chopped

Cracked black pepper

2 tablespoons lime juice, plus more as needed to taste

This salsa is the embodiment of the idea that it's important for us to eat foods that are diverse in color. It's appealing in an instinctual way—just try to look away from this beauty! Like all our salsas, this zippy one lights up even the simplest dish of quinoa, potatoes, sweet potatoes, rice, greens, or just beans. Or try it alone!

In a medium bowl, place the radishes, tomatoes, grapes, green onions, parsley, pepper, and lime juice. Mix until all the ingredients are well coated with the lime juice. Taste and add more lime juice if needed.

#1 GUACAMOLE

MAKES ABOUT 1 CUP

1 avocado

1 tablespoon Brian's Fresh Salsa (page 104) or your favorite salsa

1 clove garlic

1 teaspoon lemon juice

Once upon a time, I didn't like guacamole. But then, my pal Kristin made some and it flipped some sort of switch. Maybe being eight months pregnant and famished helped, but I recall eating the whole dish of guacamole myself. Here is that winning recipe.

In a mini food processor, place the avocado, salsa, garlic, and lemon juice and blend until well combined and creamy. (If you do not have a mini food processor, no problem! Mince or press the garlic clove through a garlic press, then place all the ingredients in a bowl and mash.)

CHAPTER 6

SANDWICH-CRAFT and BEAUTIFUL SOUPS

Keep the momentum of a healthy breakfast going with a hearty lunch or nourishing soup. We have options for big lunches, light lunches, and "out-of-the-box" lunches.

We've also included beautiful cold and warm soups. Soup combines the most wonderful and surprising ingredients. From leftovers to fresh vegetables and dried beans to fresh herbs, truly almost anything works in soup. Our soups power us at lunch or dinner to tackle the world with renewed vim and vigor. Pair a soup with any of our lunch sandwiches! Or try them with Clava Cairn Soda Bread (page 213) or Quick and Easy Beer Bread (page 205).

TUNE-IN SALAD

Heart disease-friendly

MAKES ABOUT 2 CUPS

15 ounces canned chickpeas, drained and rinsed

½ cup finely chopped celery

¼ cup finely chopped red onion

2 tablespoons chopped parsley

⅓ cup aquafaba, reserved from chickpea can

2 heaping tablespoons Dijon mustard or your favorite mustard

1 teaspoon lemon juice

½ teaspoon dried dill, or 2 teaspoons fresh dill, optional

Few pinches of dulse/seaweed flakes, optional

Ground black pepper, to taste

Yes, this recipe title sounds like tuna salad, but it tastes like a healthy twist on the tuna salad recipe we remember from days of yore. Tweak the ingredients to meet your own nostalgic recollection! Try this on an open-faced sandwich, inside a pita pocket, or in a wrap. You can add more Dijon, use less red onion, or leave out the dill. Your call. The aquafaba and mustard help create a creamy texture in this new version of an old fave.

1. Place the chickpeas into a medium bowl. With a fork, potato masher, or your hands, smash about half of them. Some chickpeas are hard to smash, and some just shed their translucent skin. Do not be deterred; it is not a pretty stage of the recipe.

2. Add the celery, onion, and parsley and stir.

3. In a small bowl, mix the aquafaba, mustard, lemon juice, dill (if using), dulse (if using), and black pepper until well combined. Pour the mustard sauce onto the chickpea mixture and stir until well coated.

VARIATION: CURRY TUNE-IN SALAD

Add 2 teaspoons curry powder and 2 teaspoons golden raisins for a curry variation.

BLT&A
and/or O
SANDWICH

To make heart disease-friendly: Use Hummus We Love (page 91) prepared without tahini (or another oil- and tahini-free hummus) or a heart disease–friendly sauce (see pages 76–77, 79–81, 84–87) and leave out the avocado

MAKES ABOUT 4

BACON TEMPEH

8 ounces tempeh

¼ cup low-sodium tamari

½ teaspoon liquid smoke

1 squirt hot sauce, your favorite

1 loaf 100% whole-grain bread

¼ cup Walnut Ginger Sauce and Dressing (page 76) or Green Goddess Sauce and Dressing (page 81)

4 ounces (about 4 handfuls) lettuce

1–2 tomatoes, sliced

1 avocado, peeled and mashed

1 onion, sliced and caramelized (page 50), optional

Bacon Tempeh, Lettuce, Tomato, and Avocado and/or Onions? Yes! Adding caramelized onions to our old favorite BLT was a pro move! And the Walnut Ginger Sauce and Dressing (page 76) or Green Goddess Sauce and Dressing (page 81) makes it a saucy winner. If you happen to have extra Bacon Tempeh, there are endless uses for it: Crumble it in BYO Bowls (page 215) or an Open-Faced Chickpea Omelet 3.0 (page 73), or add it to salads or pasta sauce. You can also use it as a layer in any sandwich or eat it simply as a side dish. We prefer butter lettuce in this sandwich, but use whatever you like!

1. Make the Bacon Tempeh: Slice the tempeh into ¼-inch-thick slices. In a large bowl, mix together the tamari, liquid smoke, hot sauce, and ¼ cup water. Add the tempeh slices to the marinade. Allow them to soak for a few minutes—the longer, the better.

2. In a nonstick pan over medium-high heat, add the tempeh and marinade. Cook for about 3 minutes, or until browned. Then, flip the slices and brown the other side. As soon as the marinade cooks off, the pan bottom becomes dry, and the tempeh browns on the second side, remove the pan from the heat.

3. Toast your bread, if desired.

4. To assemble each sandwich, spread the dressing on both slices of bread. To one slice, add the lettuce, tomato, and a few slices of Bacon Tempeh. To the other slice, add another layer of lettuce and a layer of mashed avocado and/or caramelized onions (if using). Press the two sides together and don't let go until you've devoured it and licked your fingers clean!

APPLE-LIDDED SANDWICH

To make heart disease-friendly: Use Hummus We Love (page 91) prepared without tahini (or another oil- and tahini-free hummus)

SERVES 2

3 heaping tablespoons Hummus We Love (page 91) or any oil-free hummus

2 slices 100% whole-grain bread, toasted

1–2 green onions, chopped

¼ cup roughly chopped cilantro or parsley

2 radishes or 1 watermelon radish, sliced thinly (8 large slices)

1–2 tablespoons mustard, your favorite

¼ cucumber, sliced thinly (8 large slices)

½ apple, sliced thinly from top to bottom

Lemon juice, to taste

No-salt lemon pepper (Mrs. Dash or McCormick), for garnish

Broccoli sprouts, for garnish

My brother Ted told us about this apple, cucumber, and radish sandwich he had eaten in Colorado when he was creating a mural for Denver city schools. He loved its freshness. We tried it and couldn't agree more. Ann especially loves the renegade nature of it! Such fun and so delicious. To our delight, Meg, the creator of the plant-based meal delivery service MamaSezz, tasted this sandwich, loved it, and donned it "an apple-lidded delight." We like its uniqueness, from its name to its ingredients. Just wait until you discover the difference a bite of apple makes!

1. Spread a thick layer of hummus on each slice of bread. Sprinkle with the green onions and cilantro.

2. Add the radish slices (we love the bright color of the watermelon radishes here).

3. Spread a thin layer of mustard on the bottom of each cucumber slice and then arrange on top of each radish slice.

4. Cut each sandwich in half, leaving two radishes and cucumbers on each half. Top each sandwich half with an apple slice. You can also leave the sandwich whole, especially if your apples are wide enough to cover the whole sandwich.

5. Sprinkle with the lemon juice, lemon pepper, and a garnish of sprouts. It may be messy eating but, oh, such taste and crunch.

BROOKS'S BAGEL

To make heart disease-friendly: Leave out the avocado

MAKES 2

2 whole wheat everything bagels or 100% whole-grain bagels or bread

2 teaspoons white miso

¼ sheet of nori, chopped, or a few pinches of dulse/seaweed flakes

2–3 green onions, chopped, or fresh ramps if they grow in your neck of the woods

1 avocado, mashed

1 cup spinach or spring greens

One day, we stumbled upon our friend Brooks lunching in the woods near a bed of spring ramps. He was thrilled to share his delicious sandwich with us. We had never thought to use miso as a mayo-like layer. So clever! This is now a go-to recipe—whether we are hiking or not. If you eat this messy sandwich in the woods, just wipe your hands on the ferns and keep moving.

Toast the bagels and spread a layer of miso on one side of each. Add the chopped nori onto the miso (the miso will help it stick). Sprinkle with the green onions. On the other half of the bagel, spread the mashed avocado and pile the spinach high. Carefully put both sides of the bagel together and slice in half.

ROCK-AROUND-THE-CLOCK GRILLED WRAP

To make heart disease–friendly: Use Hummus We Love (page 91) prepared without tahini (or another oil- and tahini-free hummus) and a heart disease-friendly sauce (see pages 76–77, 79–81, 84–87)

MAKES 4

4 whole-grain wraps

½ cup Hummus We Love (page 91), Thousand Island Hummus (page 93), Lemon Hummus (page 91), or any oil-free hummus

2 cups spring greens

1 tomato, sliced (or any other sliced veggies)

½ English cucumber, sliced

¼ cup Walnut Ginger Sauce and Dressing (page 76) or Lemon Tahini Sauce (page 82)

These wraps are so satisfying to fold and to eat! The flat wrap is like the face of a clock. Each quarter of the wrap represents fifteen minutes of a clock. After making an incision at the noon hour, we rock around the clock by filling each fifteen-minute section with vegetables, greens, spreads, hummuses, and sauces. Then, we fold each fifteen-minute section over the next—this process is so much fun.

We have included our favorite components below. Construct yours with your favorite vegetables, greens, and spreads. And you don't have to stick with savory ingredients! (See our suggestions for variations.)

1. Heat a panini-type sandwich grill to high heat or a pan to medium-high heat.

2. With scissors, cut a line to the center of each tortilla (remember what a radius is from geometry?).

3. Build the Rock-Around-the-Clock Grilled Wrap: Next to the incision, spread some hummus on a quarter of the wrap. It will look like you have covered the first 15 minutes of a clock.

4. In the next 15-minute section (quarter of the wrap), add the spring greens. It will look like 30 minutes of a clock are covered now. To the next 15-minute section, add the tomato slices, and to the last 15-minute section, add another layer of hummus and the cucumber slices. Drizzle the Walnut Ginger Sauce and Dressing over the greens, tomatoes, and cucumbers.

5. Now you are ready to rock around the clock and make the wrap. Fold the 15-minute section of hummus over the greens, then fold over the next 15 minutes of tomatoes, and lastly fold over the final section of hummus and cucumbers.

recipe continues

6. Place the folded wrap on the sandwich grill until crispy and grill marks form. If using a pan, flip the wrap over to get both sides crispy. However you prepare it, grab your Rock-Around-the-Clock Grilled Wrap with both hands and marvel at your creation!

VARIATIONS:

*You can make this with a lightly steamed collard green wrapper (cook for 10 seconds in a shallow pan of boiling water—steaming it makes it flexible). Load it up and fold it the same way as the whole-grain wrap, but no need to grill!

*Try a peanut butter, jam, and sliced banana version for a delicious, sweet twist!

SUMMER GARDEN OPEN-FACED SANDWICH

To make heart disease-friendly: Use Hummus We Love (page 91) prepared without tahini (or another oil- and tahini-free hummus)

SERVES 2

2 slices Mestemacher or rye bread

2 heaping tablespoons Hummus We Love (page 91) or any oil-free hummus

2 green onions, chopped

½ cup chopped purple cabbage

½ cup cooked kale or greens of choice (see page 49)

2 tablespoons lemon juice

6–8 cucumber slices

Dijon mustard or your favorite mustard

No-salt lemon pepper (Mrs. Dash or McCormick)

4–6 cherry tomatoes, halved

Handful of microgreens, sprouts, or watercress

We eat some version of this sandwich all summer long and even in the winter! Add any vegetables you choose: radishes, peppers, green onions, greens . . . experiment! We love to top it all with sprouts, microgreens, or watercress. Mestemacher bread or any thin rye works well, though whatever bread you prefer is fine. Add as much kale as you wish! It just means you need to open your mouth wider.

1. Toast the bread until crisp but not burned (it may require double toasting).

2. Spread each slice thickly with the hummus. Cover with the green onions and purple cabbage.

3. Squeeze the extra water out of the kale and spread it over the cabbage and green onions. Sprinkle the lemon juice on top of the kale.

4. Spread the bottom of all the cucumber slices with a very thin layer of mustard and place on top of the kale.

5. Sprinkle the cucumbers with *lots* of lemon pepper. Place the cherry tomatoes anywhere they will fit and top with microgreens.

6. Slice the sandwich—or not, but slicing makes it easier to eat (the cucumbers dictate where to cut it!).

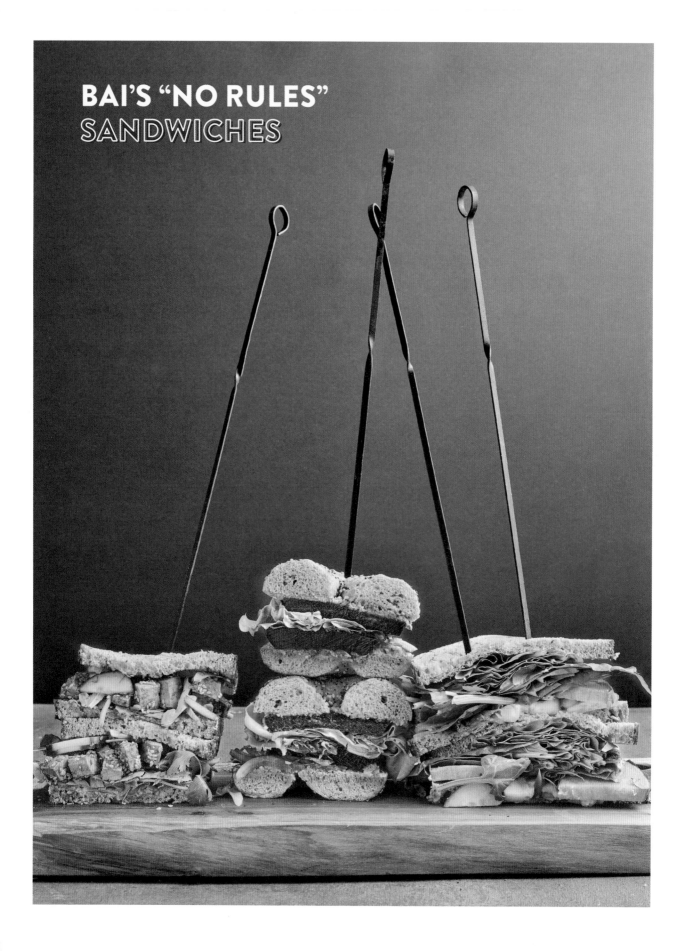

BAI'S "NO RULES" SANDWICHES

To make heart disease-friendly: Use Hummus We Love (page 91) prepared without tahini (or another oil- and tahini-free hummus) or a heart disease-friendly sauce (see pages 76–77, 79–81, 84–87) and leave out the avocado

MAKES 2

4 slices 100% whole-grain bread, 2 whole wheat pitas, or 2 whole-grain bagels

2–3 tablespoons Hummus We Love (page 91), Walnut Ginger Sauce and Dressing (page 76), Thai Peanut Sauce (page 77), Green Goddess Sauce and Dressing (page 81), Lemon Tahini Sauce (page 82), mashed avocado, or mustard

1–2 cups spring greens, romaine lettuce, spinach, or cooked kale

SPECIAL LAYER, ONE OR MORE, YOUR CALL
Cooked sliced beets

Cooked sliced sweet potatoes

Cooked tofu cubes or squares, see Tofu and Tempeh chapter (page 165)

Cooked tempeh cubes or squares

Thick slices of apple

1 tomato, sliced

½ cucumber, sliced

¼ cup cilantro, green onions, sprouts, or microgreens

Bainon is my third child and a daring plant-based eater. While we were creating this book, Bai was finishing up her senior year of high school, lifting weights in the mornings and swimming for two-plus hours in the afternoon. The boundary breaking, "out-of-the-box" sandwiches she packed left us inspired and hopeful for the next generation of Plant-Based Women Warriors. Her sandwich formula is a "sauce" such as hummus (more options below) plus a "a special layer," which she defines as a hearty plant-based middle that can be anything from sweet potato to tofu. She loves to improvise. After Thanksgiving there was no hummus for her sandwich—guess what she used instead? Mashed potatoes. Brilliant. She also makes a mean sliced sweet potato, peanut sauce, cilantro, and arugula sandwich.

Toast the bread if you wish, and spread some hummus or whatever sauce you choose on both slices. Add a thick layer of spring greens atop the hummus (this holds the greens in place). Add the "special layer" on top of the spring greens. Then, add the tomatoes, cucumbers, and cilantro. Spread a layer of hummus on the top layer of bread to help everything stay together and assemble. Slice in half and open *wide*!

ROSE'S
COLLARD
WRAPS

To make heart disease-friendly: Use Hummus We Love (page 91) prepared without tahini (or another oil- and tahini-free hummus) and serve with a heart disease–friendly dipping sauce (see pages 76–77, 79–81, 84–87)

MAKES 2

2 large collard green leaves

1 small sweet potato, cooked and mashed to the texture of hummus (see page 48), or 2–3 tablespoons Hummus We Love (page 91)

½ red bell pepper, cut into 8 thin strips

⅓ cucumber (about 4 inches), cut into 8 thin strips

½ mango, cut into 8 strips (use both halves if needed)

2 tablespoons finely chopped purple cabbage

2 radishes, sliced and cut into thin strips

Pickled ginger, optional

Arugula or cooked kale (see page 49) or broccoli sprouts

No-salt lemon pepper (Mrs. Dash or McCormick)

Thai Peanut Sauce (page 77) or Low-Fat Peanut Sauce (page 77)

These have become our latest favorite lunch thanks to my niece Rose. Ann loves the crunch and the fact that they are loaded with every possible nutrient-dense vegetable! Add roasted tofu if you so desire—it's an excellent addition, and Rose approves! The size of each wrap completely depends on the collard leaf size and the things you have in the fridge, but be careful not to make them too full. Have fun and experiment. Our favorite dipping sauce on these wraps is Thai Peanut Sauce (page 77), or Ann's favorite, Low-Fat Peanut Sauce (page 77).

1. Lay the collard greens flat on a cutting board with the shiny green side down. With a sharp knife, cut the center stem out of both collards. You will have 4 collard half-moons.

2. Spread the sweet potato mash smoothly over each leaf, leaving a few inches at the vertical top bare so you can roll it up without everything squishing out.

3. In the center of each collard half-moon, place 2 red pepper strips, 2 cucumber strips, 2 mango strips, purple cabbage, radish strips, pickled ginger (if using), arugula, and a generous sprinkle of lemon pepper.

4. Fold the bottom of the collard over the vegetables in the center and tuck the end under the vegetables and roll it up as tightly as possible to form a sausage-shaped wrap. Secure tightly with a toothpick. Dip your wraps into or drizzle them with sauce.

SUMMER CORN SLAB OPEN-FACED SANDWICH

To make heart disease-friendly: Use Hummus We Love (page 91) or Lemon Hummus (page 91) prepared without tahini (or another oil- and tahini-free hummus)

MAKES 2 OPEN-FACED SANDWICHES

2 slices Mestemacher bread or 100% whole-grain bread

4 tablespoons Hummus We Love (page 91), Lemon Hummus (page 91), or any oil-free hummus

2 green onions, chopped

¼ cup chopped purple cabbage

1 ear cooked corn on the cob or ½ cup thawed frozen corn

1 cup cooked kale (see page 49) or greens of choice

2 tablespoons lime juice

4 cherry tomatoes, halved

Zest of ½ lime

Nothing, nothing, nothing is as good as sweet summer corn. And, according to Ann, nothing is more beautiful or tastier than this sandwich. Here is a deliciously messy way to make use of any extra cooked ears of corn.

1. Toast the bread. (If you are using Mestemacher, double toast it for a crisp texture.)

2. Spread each piece of bread with the hummus and sprinkle with the green onions and purple cabbage. With a sharp knife, starting at the pointy end of the corn, slice thick slabs of corn kernels off the cob. Some of the slabs will fall apart, which is fine.

3. Put the corn on top of the cabbage, then spread the cooked greens on top of the corn.

4. Add lime juice on top of the kale—be sure to use plenty (it makes all the difference). Place the cherry tomatoes on top of the greens and sprinkle with the lime zest.

FALAFEL WRAPS, POCKETS, and SPEARS

To make heart disease-friendly: Use Hummus We Love (page 91) prepared without tahini (or another oil- and tahini-free hummus) or a heart disease-friendly sauce (see pages 76–77, 79–81, 84–87)

MAKES ABOUT 20

1½ cups chickpea flour

15 ounces canned chickpeas, drained and rinsed

15 ounces canned black beans, drained and rinsed

½ red onion, diced

2 large cloves garlic, minced

½ cup roughly chopped parsley leaves and stems

½ cup roughly chopped cilantro leaves and stems, optional

2 teaspoons cumin

2 teaspoons coriander

2 teaspoons lemon juice

1 tablespoon tomato paste

1 teaspoon hot sauce, your favorite

½ teaspoon turmeric

¼ teaspoon red pepper flakes

Pinch of cinnamon, optional

½ teaspoon salt, optional

Ground black pepper, to taste

Falafel patties are traditionally deep fried, but we used to feel, well, awful after eating falafel that had been prepared this way. Now, we are thrilled about our no-oil baked versions, which are just as yummy as traditional falafel patties and packed with powerful delicious ingredients—yet they don't leave us feeling gross and groggy! Baked falafel works in wraps, pita pockets, or on spears of romaine with Hummus We Love (page 91) and some red onion, parsley, cilantro, and tomatoes. Or try serving them with Cool Cucumber Soup (page 131).

Falafel's unique flavor is in the seasonings, so tweak the spices according to where your falafel love lies: more cumin, more lemon, less garlic, or even a pinch of cinnamon—your call.

1. Preheat the oven to 350°F. Line a sheet pan with parchment paper.

2. To a food processor or high-speed blender, add the chickpea flour, chickpeas, black beans, onion, garlic, parsley, cilantro (if using), cumin, coriander, lemon juice, tomato paste, hot sauce, turmeric, red pepper flakes, cinnamon (if using), salt (if using), and black pepper. Pulse until the ingredients are combined yet still have some texture, adding a tablespoon of water if needed. The mixture should look and feel like thick, textured hummus.

3. Using a spoon and your hands, form patties with about 2 tablespoons batter per patty. (Wetting your fingers helps keep the batter from sticking.) Place the patties on the prepared pan. Bake for 15 minutes, remove from the oven, flip, and bake for 15 more minutes. The falafel patties will be slightly browned and firm, yet soft inside. Serve immediately.

COOL CUCUMBER SOUP

Heart disease-friendly

SERVES 2-4

4 medium cucumbers or
1 very large cucumber
(about 4 cups), chopped

½ cup whole fresh mint
leaves, plus more for garnish

Zest of 1 lime

2 tablespoons lime juice

2 teaspoons white miso

½ teaspoon ground black
pepper

Pinch of cayenne pepper

2 whole oranges, peeled and
seeded, or ⅔ cup orange juice

This easy soup solves the "too many cucumbers" problem we often have for a few weeks every summer. It is incredibly satisfying on a day that is simply too hot to even consider cooking! If you use cold cucumbers, it is ready to relieve the heat in a flash. By adding the oranges or orange juice at the end, the soup stays a lovely green. The soup is so good it even works as a salad dressing—just add balsamic vinegar (see page 95).

1. In a high-speed blender, place the cucumber, mint, lime zest, lime juice, miso, black pepper, and cayenne pepper and blend until well combined. Add the oranges and keep blending until smooth.

2. Refrigerate until chilled and serve with mint leaves on top and thick summer tomato sandwiches for a beautiful lunch.

CORN GAZPACHO

Heart disease-friendly

SERVES 4-6

1 cucumber

3 ears sweet corn
(about 2¼ cups of kernels) or
16 ounces frozen sweet corn,
plus a few kernels for garnish

1 orange bell pepper,
roughly chopped

½ sweet onion, chopped

1 cup chopped yellow or
orange tomatoes or about
12 orange or yellow cherry
tomatoes

2 pinches red pepper flakes or
¼ jalapeño pepper

2–3 tablespoons red wine
vinegar, to taste

½ teaspoon ground black
pepper, or to taste

12 halved cherry tomatoes,
for garnish

2 chopped green onions
or chives, or microgreens,
for garnish, optional

One of our oldest friends, Elizabeth, raved about this recipe from her home in Santa Fe. After we managed to persuade her to share it with us, we hit a local farmers market and found all the produce we needed! Wait until you try this sweet deliciousness. Use the sweetest corn you can possibly find! We swooned as Elizabeth had predicted. We serve a winning combination of this soup with Brooks's Bagel (page 117). This is even good a day or so after you make it.

1. Cut the cucumber in half lengthwise (peeling is optional) and remove the seeds if they are big. Chop roughly and place in a food processor. Add the corn, bell pepper, onion, tomato, red pepper flakes, vinegar, and black pepper and blend until smooth. If you like a chunky texture, blend until it reaches your desired consistency.

2. Serve with corn kernels, halved cherry tomatoes, and chopped green onions, chives, or microgreens (if using) on top. Or just eat plain spoonfuls out of the food processor.

NEW SENATE SOUP

Heart disease–friendly

SERVES 8–10

1 pound dried navy beans

1 bay leaf

4 cups vegetable stock

2 Yukon Gold (or yellow) potatoes, diced

2 stalks celery, chopped

1 large onion, chopped

2 large cloves garlic, minced

1 red bell pepper, diced

1 cup canned black beans, drained and rinsed

¼ cup Italian parsley, chopped

2 cups curly kale, loosely packed, stems removed, chopped

¼ teaspoon kosher salt, optional

Ground black pepper, to taste

2 squirts hot sauce, or to taste (we prefer sriracha)

The Senate Bean Soup recipe has been around since the early twentieth century, and it is apparently still on the menu every day at the restaurant within the US Senate. The Senate has changed a great deal in the last century, and so we created a new version of the old soup—one that reflects the diversity, flavor, and strength of today's Senate. We replaced the ham bone and meat with vegetable stock and bay leaf, then rounded out the new flavor with black beans, red pepper, hot sauce, "curvy" kale, Italian parsley, and kosher salt (optional). We love this creamy soup—and we hope friends on both sides of the aisle will as well. Take turns serving yourself with a ladle, as though it's a gavel!

Try serving this with the Rock-Around-the-Clock Grilled Wrap (page 119).

1. Place the navy beans in a large pot with the bay leaf, vegetable stock, 8 cups water, the potatoes, celery, onion, and garlic. Bring to a boil over high heat, then reduce the heat to low and cook until the potatoes dissolve and the beans are tender, 1½ to 2 hours.

2. With an immersion blender, pulse the soup so it is half creamy and half textured. (You can also transfer half of the soup to a food processor or high-speed blender and blend until creamy, and then pour it back into the soup pot.)

3. To the soup pot, add the red pepper, black beans, parsley, and kale and stir. Continue simmering for another 30 minutes. If the soup gets too thick, add more water. Season with salt (if using), black pepper, and hot sauce.

LOADED VEGETABLE SOUP
with FARRO and BEANS

Heart disease-friendly

SERVES 6

1 large onion, chopped

2 large stalks celery, chopped (about 1 cup)

3 carrots, chopped in ½-inch pieces (about 1 cup)

2 teaspoons fresh thyme or 1 teaspoon dried

3 cloves garlic, minced (about 1 tablespoon)

6 ounces tomato paste

20 grape or cherry tomatoes, halved (about 1 cup)

8 cups low-sodium vegetable broth

1 cup uncooked farro

15 ounces canned kidney beans or beans of choice, drained and rinsed

2 tablespoons white miso

½ cup fresh basil leaves, coarsely chopped

½ teaspoon ground black pepper

1 cup frozen peas

1 cup frozen corn

4–8 ounces spinach, or more to taste

2 tablespoons balsamic vinegar (see page 95)

Parsley, chopped, for garnish

This is such a satisfying soup—it is loaded with everything you want to eat in a day! Add more vegetables at the end if you wish, a whole package of frozen mixed vegetables or anything in your fridge or freezer. Add hot sauce, lemon juice, or balsamic vinegar to taste, or eat just as it is. Serve with a warm loaf of Quick and Easy Beer Bread (page 205)—so good!

1. In a large pot over medium-high heat, add 2 tablespoons water. Place the onion, celery, carrots, and thyme in the pot and stir until the vegetables begin to soften, about 10 minutes.

2. Add the garlic and tomato paste and stir to combine.

3. Add the grape tomatoes and vegetable broth and bring to a boil over high heat.

4. Add the farro and beans, reduce the heat to a simmer, cover, and cook for 25 minutes, or until the farro is tender.

5. Add the miso, basil, pepper, peas, corn, and spinach. Stir in the balsamic vinegar and continue stirring while the spinach wilts beautifully. Garnish with the parsley.

NEW YEAR'S PARSNIP SOUP

Heart disease-friendly

SERVES 8–10

1 large onion, chopped (2–3 cups)

6 cloves garlic, chopped

4–5 cups low-sodium vegetable broth

1 butternut squash, peeled and cubed (about 6 cups)

4 parsnips, chopped (about 6 cups)

2 tablespoons fresh thyme or 1 tablespoon dried

1–2 tablespoons lemon juice, to taste

½–1 teaspoon ground black pepper, to taste

½ pound spinach or Swiss chard, roughly chopped

¼–½ cup coarsely chopped cilantro or parsley

A neighbor of ours has a soup party every New Year's Day and usually makes seven different varieties for everyone to sample. One year, the vegetarian offering was a parsnip soup made with butternut squash, parsnips, thyme, and onion. We made it the next day and used sweet potato since we didn't have a butternut squash and added garlic and *lots* of spinach and cilantro. We loved it just as much! If you are using butternut squash, an easy option is to buy it peeled and cut at the grocery store. Serve this soup with Rose's Collard Wraps (page 124) for a delicious and colorful lunch!

1. In a large pot over medium-high heat, cook the onion while stirring until it is translucent and just beginning to brown, about 5 minutes (add water as needed to avoid burning).

2. Add the garlic and stir briefly. Then, add the vegetable broth, butternut squash, parsnips, and thyme and bring to a boil. Reduce the heat to a simmer and cook for 30 minutes, or until the vegetables are tender.

3. Transfer the soup in batches to a blender and blend until smooth. Or use an immersion blender right in the pot.

4. Add the lemon juice and pepper, and just before serving add the spinach and cilantro.

TIP:
To soften the butternut squash so it is easier to cube, microwave for 4 to 5 minutes, or purchase cubed butternut squash.

AFRICAN PEANUT SOUP

SOUP

SERVES 6

1 medium onion, diced

2 stalks celery, chopped

1 medium carrot, chopped

1 tablespoon minced fresh ginger

3 cloves garlic, minced

2 teaspoons curry powder

3 cups vegetable broth

8 ounces sweet potatoes, cut into 1-inch pieces

1 tomato, diced

⅓ cup peanut butter

15 ounces canned black beans or beans of choice, drained and rinsed

½ cup oat milk or any nondairy milk

Cilantro, roughly chopped, for garnish

This creamy, nutrient-packed soup came our way in the best fashion. From next door! Our next-door neighbor, Susie, adapted it from a newsletter and goodness knows where they got it. Share this soup with your neighbor and let's keep paying it forward.

1. In a large pot over medium-high heat, heat 2 tablespoons water. Add the onion, celery, carrot, ginger, and garlic and cook, stirring, until the onion becomes translucent and softened, about 4 minutes. Stir in the curry powder until everything appears coated with curry. Add the vegetable broth, sweet potatoes, and tomato and bring to a boil. Reduce the heat to medium-low and add the peanut butter, beans, and oat milk and simmer for about 15 minutes.

2. With an immersion blender, pulse the soup so it is half creamy and half textured. (You can also transfer half of the soup to a food processor or high-speed blender and blend until creamy, and then pour it back into the soup pot.) Garnish with the cilantro and serve.

CARROT MUSHROOM RED LENTIL SOUP

Heart disease-friendly

SERVES 4

1 large onion, chopped

6 cloves garlic, chopped

½ teaspoon cumin

1 teaspoon chili powder

½ teaspoon turmeric

Pinch of cayenne pepper, or to taste

¼ teaspoon ground black pepper

6 ounces tomato paste

6 cups vegetable broth

1½ cups dried red lentils

4–5 large carrots, diced (about 4 cups)

2–4 cups Swiss chard or beet greens, including stems, or greens of choice

8–16 ounces mushrooms, sliced, use more or less depending on your love for mushrooms

Zest of ½ lemon

2 tablespoons lemon juice

1 tablespoon balsamic vinegar (see page 95)

1 cup cilantro or parsley, roughly chopped, for garnish

The color of this soup wins us over. Make it your own by adding the amount of lemon, cilantro, and spices you like! Try to buy Swiss chard with the red stems, which will help give this soup a vibrant warm hue. In fact, the soup is so good that we usually double the recipe. And we make a double batch of Clava Cairn Soda Bread (page 213) for dipping.

1. In a large pot over medium heat, add 2 tablespoons water. Add the onion and cook until it becomes translucent and softened, about 5 minutes, adding more water if necessary.

2. Stir in the garlic, cumin, chili powder, turmeric, cayenne pepper, and black pepper. Add the tomato paste and cook another minute or two.

3. Add the vegetable broth, lentils, and carrots, and bring to a boil. Reduce the heat to a simmer, partially cover, and cook for about 10 minutes, or until the lentils and carrots start to soften.

4. Add the Swiss chard and mushrooms and simmer, covered, another 20 minutes.

5. We like this soup chunky, but if you wish, you can puree it with an immersion blender right in the pot or transfer some of the soup to a blender. Stir in the lemon zest, lemon juice, and balsamic vinegar before serving. Garnish with the cilantro.

28 Oct 23   okay

BIG BEAN BARLEY and SWEET POTATO SOUP

Heart disease-friendly

SERVES 6

1 cup sliced shallots (about 2 large), or 1 onion, sliced

4 cloves garlic, chopped

1 tablespoon minced fresh ginger

1 teaspoon dried rosemary

6 cups vegetable broth

1 large skin-on sweet potato, cubed into about ¾-inch pieces

½ cup barley or farro

⅛ teaspoon cayenne pepper

2 cups cooked large lima beans or 15 ounces canned kidney beans, drained and rinsed

1 bunch red-stemmed Swiss chard including stems, chopped, or other greens of choice

1 tablespoon maple syrup, optional

1 tablespoon white miso

1 tablespoon balsamic vinegar (see page 95)

This soup comes to us from my sister-in-law, Polly, by way of vegan chef Isa Chandra Moskowitz. We've made this hearty recipe our own over time with our usual tweaks of different greens, a variety of beans, and Ann's favorite—balsamic vinegar! The large lima beans make it so good. Royal Corona Beans from Rancho Gordo (RanchoGordo.com) are creamy and delicious and so worth finding! Otherwise, you can use large lima beans or even kidney beans. Note: If using dried beans in this recipe, cook them in advance.

1. In a large pot over medium-high heat, add 2 tablespoons water. Add the shallots and cook until they become translucent, about 3 minutes, adding more water if necessary.

2. Stir in the garlic, ginger, and rosemary and continue cooking for about 30 seconds.

3. Add the vegetable broth, sweet potato, barley, and cayenne pepper and bring just to a boil.

4. Reduce the heat to a simmer and cook, partially covered, 15 to 20 minutes, until the sweet potato is just tender.

5. Add the lima beans, Swiss chard, and maple syrup (if using) and cook about 3 minutes, until the Swiss chard begins to soften.

6. In a small bowl, place some of the soup liquid and stir in the miso. Add to the pot and stir in the balsamic vinegar.

1 NOV 23 o Unusual taste. Good. But thin.

CHAPTER 7

WARRIOR

Some people think following a plant-based diet means that all you eat is salad. By no means is this true! We eat a huge variety of food. Yet we *do* love to create massive, colorful, complex, delicious bowls that hit the *salad* nail on the head: crisp cabbages and kale, fresh green onions, fresh bright radishes, sweet berries, toasted pepitas, and a winning dressing. Right on! When the bowl is this luscious, all we want to eat is salad. Heck, we may not even want to share it!

THREE GODDESSES SALAD

To make heart disease-friendly: Do not add walnuts

SERVES 8

½ bunch kale, stems stripped and leaves chiffonade cut (about 2 cups)

1 head romaine, chopped

½ napa cabbage, chiffonade cut (1½–2 cups)

½ purple cabbage, finely chopped

½ cucumber, sliced

3–4 green onions, chopped, to taste

1½ cups blueberries, or more to taste

3–4 clementines, peeled, sectioned, membrane removed, and sliced (see note, page 159), or 10 ounces canned mandarin oranges, drained

1 cup walnut pieces, raw or toasted

1 cup pepitas (pumpkin seeds), raw or toasted

Greens rule this salad for different reasons: Kale is Athena, the battle strategist—fighting free radicals, inflammation, and disease with her thick, protective skin. Romaine is Isis, the magical protector of women and children, always fresh no matter how long she has been in your fridge, and her taste appeals to kids. Napa cabbage is Ceridwen, the shapeshifter, ready for whatever the need—it can be raw or cooked, on a top or bottom layer, or mixed in throughout! Take comfort in serving this salad with its protective pantheon of phytochemicals and flavors. Baritone Dressing (page 97) or Crile's Light Lemon Dressing (page 98) are our favorite dressings with Three Goddesses Salad.

In a large salad bowl, combine the kale, romaine, napa cabbage, purple cabbage, cucumber, green onions, blueberries, clementines, walnuts, and pepitas. Toss with your favorite dressing and feel the protection and magic!

WONDER WOMAN SALAD

To make heart disease-friendly: Use pumpkin seeds instead of pecans and leave out the avocado

SERVES 6

1 head romaine, chopped

1 bunch kale, leaves stripped off stems and chopped

1 cup cubed apple

1 cup cherry tomatoes, halved

1 red bell pepper, diced

3–4 green onions, chopped

1 avocado, diced, optional

½ cup pecans, toasted until fragrant

This salad holds nothing back! It makes us Wonder Women: brave, strong, clear headed, and clear boweled. A wonder indeed! Try this with Walnut Horseradish Dressing (page 99), Lightning Dressing (page 101), or 3-2-1 Hum Dressing (page 97).

In a large salad bowl, combine the romaine, kale, apple, tomatoes, red pepper, green onions, avocado (if using), and pecans. Toss with your favorite dressing.

RAINBOW BEAN SLAW

Heart disease–friendly

SERVES 4

2 cups shredded or very finely chopped cabbage, a mix of colors if possible

15 ounces canned no-salt black beans, drained and rinsed

1 red bell pepper, chopped

¼–½ cup chopped green onions

½ cup cherry tomatoes, halved

½ cup cilantro, chopped, optional

Zest and juice of 1 lime (at least 2 tablespoons juice)

2–3 tablespoons white balsamic vinegar (see page 95) or dressing of your choice

This slaw is a burst of color visually as well as a burst of taste in your mouth! And it is so *easy* if you buy shredded cabbage (some stores offer a multicolored coleslaw mix with carrots).

It is good on a bed of arugula, inside a baked spaghetti squash, and absolutely *delicious* on top of cheeseless pizza! Try it and you'll never eat pizza without salad on top again.

In a medium bowl, mix the cabbage, black beans, red pepper, green onions, tomatoes, cilantro (if using), lime zest, lime juice, and balsamic vinegar and allow to sit a few minutes before eating so the flavors can mingle. It's hard not to eat it right away because it looks so fresh and appealing!

PERSEPHONE HOLIDAY SALAD

Heart disease-friendly

SERVES 4

1 bunch kale, stems stripped and leaves finely chopped

1 heaping tablespoon Hummus We Love (page 91) or any oil-free hummus

2 cups whole brussels sprouts

½ cup dressing of your choice

3–4 clementines, peeled, sectioned, membrane removed, and halved (see note, page 159)

½ cup pomegranate seeds (see note)

In the dark of winter, around the shortest days of the year, we serve our Persephone Salad so that we can talk about the myth of Demeter, Persephone, and Hades. We love retelling how Demeter, the goddess of growing things, loses her daughter to the underworld and the crazy role a pomegranate plays in it all! Pomegranates are in season during the colder months. Don't forget to bring notes about the myth to the table when serving this salad. We recommend enjoying this with Ann and Essy's Favorite Dressing (page 96) or Lightning Dressing (page 101).

1. In a large salad bowl, combine the kale and hummus. Massage the kale well with your hands to soften. It will take a few minutes. Squeeze hard!

2. In a food processor, place the brussels sprouts and process until well shredded, about a minute. Add to the bowl with the kale. The bright green kale and lighter green brussels sprouts will look beautiful at this stage.

3. Add the dressing and mix well. Add the clementines and the pomegranate seeds and toss to combine.

NOTE:

To remove the seeds from the pomegranate, fill a medium bowl with water, cut the pomegranate in quarters, and remove the seeds into the bowl with your hands. The white pith will float and the seeds will sink. Skim off the pith with your hands or a small strainer, and then drain the seeds. You will have more than ½ cup. Add them all if you wish or save some for another use. They are delicious to eat just on their own.

BRIGHT QUINOA LIME MINT SALAD

Heart disease–friendly

SERVES 4

2 cups cooked quinoa
or any cooked grain
(brown rice, barley, or farro)

½ red bell pepper, diced

1 cup fresh or thawed frozen
peas

1 mango, diced

¼ cup raisins

¼ cup diced red onion

⅓ cup chiffonade-cut fresh
mint, optional

⅓ cup chopped fresh parsley

Zest of 1 lime

3 tablespoons lime juice

2 tablespoons white balsamic
vinegar (see page 95)

This beautiful salad tastes as good as it looks, bright and light and flavorful. Serve it alone, on a bed of greens, or as filling in a pita pocket, collard leaf, or romaine spear. If peas aren't your thing, add celery. If mint isn't your thing, no problem, try fresh basil. It's summer in a bowl!

1. In a large bowl, combine the cooked quinoa, red pepper, peas, mango, raisins, onion, mint (if using), and parsley.

2. Stir in the lime zest, lime juice, and vinegar.

CURRIED CAULIFLOWER SALAD with LENTILS and GRAPES

Heart disease-friendly

SERVES 4–6

1 head cauliflower, cut into small florets

1½ tablespoons curry powder

1 tablespoon green curry paste

2 tablespoons lemon juice

2 tablespoons Hummus We Love (page 91) or any oil-free hummus

1 tablespoon lemon white balsamic vinegar (see page 95)

Ground black pepper, to taste

5–6 cups arugula or greens of choice

1½ cups cooked lentils (about ½ cup dry lentils)

1½–2 cups red or green grapes, halved

The idea for this dish comes from the *Minimalist Baker* blog. We made it for Thanksgiving with our usual modifications, and it was the first dish completely devoured on our bountiful table. The larger the grapes, the better in this dish, and either green or red is delicious. Tip: Add pomegranate seeds for wonderful color at the end.

1. Preheat the oven to 400°F. Line a sheet pan with parchment paper.

2. In a large bowl, gently combine the cauliflower with the curry powder and 2 tablespoons water.

3. Spread the cauliflower on the prepared pan and roast for 20 to 25 minutes, until golden brown and tender.

4. Make the dressing: In a small bowl, mix together the green curry paste, lemon juice, hummus, vinegar, and pepper until well combined.

5. To assemble the salad, place the greens in a wide bowl and top with the lentils and grapes and then the cauliflower. Pour dressing over the salad, show off how beautiful it looks, then toss and eat it up.

ORANGE MANGO BEAN SALAD

Heart disease-friendly

SERVES 4

15 ounces canned cannellini beans (about 1½ cups), canned navy beans, or cooked large lima beans, drained and rinsed

1–2 mangoes (about 1½ cups), peeled and diced

2 navel oranges (about 1½ cups), peeled, sectioned, membrane removed, and cubed (see note, page 159)

1–2 teaspoons minced jalapeño pepper

2 teaspoons lime zest (from 1½–2 limes)

¼ cup lime juice, or more to taste

2 tablespoons chopped fresh mint

5–6 cups arugula or greens of choice

This salad sings with a melody of bright, zesty, flavorful ingredients. It is fabulous on a bed of arugula, mâche, or mesclun mix, or try it tucked into romaine, Bibb lettuce, or pita bread. It is especially wonderful with the large lima beans from Rancho Gordo. Note: If using dried beans in this recipe, cook them in advance.

In a large bowl, combine the beans, mangoes, oranges, jalapeño, lime zest and juice, and mint. Do a quick taste test to see if you need more lime juice. Arrange the arugula or greens of choice in the bottom of a wide bowl, add the bean mixture, and feast on a combination of such good tastes!

ANN'S ARUGULA SALAD SECTION

Arugula has the most potent endothelial cell–enhancing powers of all the greens, and so Ann tries to use it in her cooking whenever possible. She also uses premium-quality white balsamic or a lemon white balsamic vinegar (see page 95) in her arugula salads, which she says makes all the difference. These salads are also delicious with our Strawberry Balsamic Dressing (page 99).

ANN'S ARUGULA and
FANCY BEET SALAD

**ANN'S ARUGULA
GRAPEFRUIT
STRAWBERRY
SALAD**

**ANN'S ARUGULA
and GORGEOUS
CITRUS SALAD**

ANN'S ARUGULA and
**BRIGHT ORANGE
SALAD** with **DILL**

ANN'S ARUGULA *and* GORGEOUS CITRUS SALAD

Heart disease–friendly

Once, when we received a gift box full of oranges and grapefruit, we knew we had to be creative to use them up. So, we created this gorgeous, breathtaking, colorful salad. It is convenient, though expensive, to buy pomegranates already seeded, but really the fun is to remove them yourself (see note, page 152). Best of all, this salad needs *no* dressing other than a squeeze of lemon, though the raspberry white balsamic vinegar adds a delicious taste.

SERVES 2

2 cups arugula

1 cup microgreens

1 ruby red grapefruit, peeled, sectioned, membrane removed, and cut into bite-size pieces (see note)

2 oranges, peeled, sectioned, membrane removed, and cut into bite-size pieces (see note)

½ cup pomegranate seeds (see note, page 152)

½ cup raspberries

1 tablespoon lemon juice

2 tablespoons white or raspberry white balsamic vinegar (see page 95), optional

Fresh mint, chopped or whole leaves, for garnish

Arrange the arugula and microgreens in a medium salad bowl, add the grapefruit and orange sections and juice on top, and sprinkle the pomegranate seeds and raspberries over the whole bowl.

Sprinkle with the lemon juice and stir in the vinegar (if using). Garnish with the mint.

NOTE:

To prepare the fruit, cut both ends off the grapefruit and oranges, removing the pith as well. Over a small bowl to catch the drippings, peel the grapefruit and oranges, again removing the pith (you may be able to do it in one peel). Cut out one section, then slide the remaining sections off into the salad bowl and continue cutting and sliding all the sections until just the fibrous sections are left in your hand. Squeeze any remaining juice into the bowl.

ANN'S ARUGULA *and* FANCY BEET SALAD

To make heart disease–friendly: Do not add walnuts

Beets are powerhouses for enhancing endothelial function. For beet lovers (and beet lovers to be), here is a delicious way to eat more of them. Try this salad with In the Pink Dressing (page 100) and you will be hooked on beets!

SERVES 2–3

3 medium beets, cooked, cooled, peeled, and sliced

¼ cup orange juice

2 tablespoons white or lemon white balsamic vinegar (page 95)

2 cups arugula

Cracked black pepper, to taste

¼ cup walnut pieces, toasted, optional

In a small bowl, gently combine the beets, orange juice, and vinegar.

Place the arugula in a medium salad bowl and add the beets and a crack of black pepper.

Garnish with the toasted walnuts (if using).

ANN'S ARUGULA *and* BRIGHT ORANGE SALAD *with* DILL

Heart disease-friendly

Here is a parade of flavor: dill, orange, and summer's finest cucumbers. It's tasty just as it is and even more amazing with Strawberry Balsamic Dressing (page 99).

SERVES 3–4

½ cucumber, sliced (not necessary to peel!)

2 navel oranges, peeled, sectioned, membrane removed, and cut into bite-size pieces (see note, page 159)

2 tablespoons chopped fresh dill

1 tablespoon chiffonade-cut fresh mint

½ teaspoon dried thyme

½ teaspoon dried rosemary

Zest of ½ lemon

1 tablespoon lemon juice

2 cups arugula

In a small bowl, gently combine the cucumber, orange sections and juice, 1 tablespoon of the dill, the mint, thyme, rosemary, lemon zest, and lemon juice.

In a medium salad bowl, arrange the arugula so some comes up the side. Add the cucumber mixture and sprinkle with the remaining tablespoon of fresh dill.

ANN'S ARUGULA GRAPEFRUIT STRAWBERRY SALAD

Heart disease-friendly

This lovely combination of ingredients brings summer's abundance to a dark winter day and perfection to a steamy summer meal. Although unnecessary, Strawberry Balsamic Dressing (page 99) highlights this salad if you want a dressing.

SERVES 2

1 grapefruit, peeled, sectioned, membrane removed, and cut into bite-size pieces (see note, page 159)

8 grapes, halved

4 large strawberries, sliced

1–2 tablespoons raspberry or white balsamic vinegar (see page 95), to taste

2 cups arugula

½ cup raspberries

In a small bowl, combine the grapefruit sections and juice, grapes, strawberries, and vinegar.

In a medium salad bowl, arrange the arugula so some comes up the side. Add the grapefruit, grapes, and strawberries and sprinkle the raspberries over the top.

CHAPTER 8

TOFU and TEMPEH, TASTY ADDITIONS

Tofu and tempeh add satisfaction and complexity to a simple light lunch or a hearty dinner feast. We enjoy them plain in our Black Ramen Bowl (page 247) and Plant-Based Pad Thai (page 255), or beautifully layered with flavor and spice in the BYO Buddha Bowl (page 221) and Groove-On Quinoa Bowl (page 233). And oh what a joy it is to find leftover tofu or tempeh cubes the next day—inspiring! You can throw them into salads, enjoy them with a heaping side of roasted vegetables, and so much more. Play around!

Knowing the best type of tofu to purchase is key. We highly suggest organic, non-GMO firm, extra-firm, or super-firm tofu for the

continues

recipes in this section. This type of tofu is often sold in a tub or wrapped in plastic in the refrigerated section. Honestly, the firmer the better for tofu cubes in a dinner or lunch dish.

A note about tofu preparation: If you are using firm or extra-firm tofu for these recipes, consider using a tofu press to remove excess water before cooking, so that the tofu will soak up the seasonings better. Too much liquid in tofu may dilute the flavor you work hard to achieve! Super-firm tofu does not need to be pressed.

Don't have a tofu press? No problem, neither do we. Instead, we wrap our tofu in a number of dish towels (sometimes, we slice the block of tofu longways to create two thinner tofu blocks) and apply gentle pressure by placing cutting boards or heavy books on top. We let the tofu sit for an hour or so, then cube it and toss with any of the marinades or mixtures in this chapter.

In our dessert section (page 273), we often use silken firm tofu, which is a different beast altogether. It makes luscious and creamy frostings, puddings, and gelatos, and it falls apart when handled.

BASIC BAKED TOFU CUBES

Heart disease–friendly

MAKES ABOUT 2 CUPS

12 ounces firm or extra-firm tofu, pressed (see page 166) and cut into ½-inch cubes

¼ cup low-sodium tamari

2 tablespoons maple syrup, optional

This tofu recipe is a basic component of many of our BYO Bowl dinners. It is simple, it is bolstering, it is delish. If you want the cubes to have more luster, add 2 tablespoons maple syrup to the tamari. If not, leave it out.

1. Preheat the oven to 400°F. Line a sheet pan with parchment paper.

2. In a medium bowl, combine the tofu cubes with the tamari and maple syrup (if using). Toss the cubes until well coated. If you have the time, allow the cubes to marinate for a few minutes.

3. Pour the tofu cubes and any extra liquid onto the prepared pan, spreading in a single layer. Bake for 20 to 30 minutes, until browned to your liking.

BASIC PAN-FRIED TEMPEH CUBES

Heart disease–friendly

MAKES ABOUT 2 CUPS

8 ounces tempeh, cut into ½-inch cubes

¼ cup low-sodium tamari

¼ teaspoon liquid smoke, optional

Some love tempeh, some love tofu, we love both. And both liven up the BYO Bowl dinners we love to have at our house. While we prefer our tofu baked, we like our tempeh pan fried as it keeps the tempeh moist. But if you like fried tofu, you can cook them this way, too!

In a medium bowl, combine the tempeh cubes with the tamari and liquid smoke (if using). Once the cubes are coated, allow them to soak up the tamari, from 2 to 20 minutes, depending on how much time you have. In a large nonstick pan over medium-high heat, pour in the tempeh and sauce and stir, allowing the cubes to cook on all sides. The key here is to keep an eye on the heat and turn it down as soon as the tamari starts to bubble and burn off. Add 1 teaspoon of water, if needed, to loosen the tamari from the bottom of the pan (otherwise it sticks like cement!). The tempeh is ready once it is browned and warmed to your liking, around 4 minutes.

TERIYAKI TOFU or TEMPEH CUBES

Heart disease–friendly

MAKES ABOUT 2 CUPS

½ cup low-sodium tamari

¼ cup maple syrup

3 tablespoons ketchup or tomato paste

1 tablespoon minced fresh ginger

¼ cup toasted sesame seeds

12 ounces firm or extra-firm tofu, pressed (see page 166), or 12 ounces tempeh, cut into ½-inch cubes

These are a knock-your-socks-off favorite for all family gatherings. They are also the most requested meal for birthday parties. We love how simple these little bites are to prepare, yet they still add a little cha-cha-cha to the meal.

1. Make the teriyaki sauce: In a medium bowl, combine the tamari, maple syrup, ketchup, ginger, and sesame seeds. Set aside about ¼ cup teriyaki sauce to use as a sauce on top! Add the tofu or tempeh cubes to the remaining sauce and toss until well coated.

2. For tofu cubes: Preheat the oven to 400°F. Line a sheet pan with parchment paper.

3. Allow the cubes to marinate for a few minutes if you have the time.

4. Pour the tofu cubes and any extra liquid onto the sheet pan, spreading them out in a single layer. Bake for 20 to 30 minutes, until browned to your liking.

5. For tempeh cubes: Once the cubes are coated, allow them to soak up the teriyaki sauce, from 2 to 20 minutes, depending on how much time you have.

6. In a large nonstick pan over medium-high heat, pour in the tempeh and sauce, and cook the cubes on all sides. The key here is to keep an eye on the heat and turn it down as the sauce starts to bubble and burn off. Add teaspoons of water, if needed, to remove the tempeh and sauce from the bottom of the pan. It is ready once it is browned and warmed to your liking, around 4 minutes.

SESAME GINGER-TOPPED TOFU or TEMPEH

Heart disease-friendly

MAKES ABOUT 2 CUPS

¼ cup low-sodium tamari

2 tablespoons maple syrup

2 tablespoons rice vinegar

12 ounces extra-firm tofu, pressed (see page 166), or 12 ounces tempeh, cut into ¼-inch-thick square slabs (the size of pats of butter) or triangles

2 pinches red pepper flakes

2 cloves garlic, minced

1 inch fresh ginger, minced

2 tablespoons black sesame seeds

2–3 green onions, thinly sliced

My kids love the Happy Pear lads almost as much as I do. They are chronically appealing vegan twins, Steven and David Flynn, from Ireland, and the kids found inspiration for this recipe watching the twins' YouTube tofu video! These satisfying squares pack layers of flavor and fragrance—so much so, we often eat them alone. The toasted sesame seeds, garlic, and ginger really send us all over the hedge! Mmm! Add these to your BYO Buddha Bowl (page 221), salad, or sandwich.

1. In a medium bowl, combine the tamari, maple syrup, and rice vinegar. Place the tofu or tempeh into the sauce and stir until well coated. Allow to marinate for a few minutes if time allows.

2. Heat a large nonstick pan over medium-high heat. Working in batches if necessary, lay the tofu or tempeh slabs in a single layer in the pan and pour in any extra sauce. Watch closely, and just as the liquid cooks off, remove the pan from the heat.

3. Prepare the topping: In a nonstick pan over medium heat, cook the red pepper flakes, garlic, and ginger until fragrant, 2 to 3 minutes. Add the sesame seeds and cook and stir for another few minutes, until the sesame seeds also get fragrant. Add the green onions, stir and cook for a minute, and remove from the heat.

4. Place the beautifully browned tofu or tempeh in a serving dish and cover with the sesame ginger topping. Serve over brown rice, with salads, or in sandwiches.

CHORIZO TEMPEH or TOFU

Heart disease–friendly

MAKES 2½–3 CUPS

3 tablespoons chili powder

1 tablespoon garlic powder

1 teaspoon cumin

½ teaspoon turmeric

1 tablespoon dried oregano

½ teaspoon smoked paprika

4 grinds black pepper

¼ cup apple cider vinegar

2 tablespoons low-sodium tamari

2 cups diced onion

12 ounces tempeh or 12 ounces firm or extra-firm tofu, pressed (see page 166), crumbled or diced

½ teaspoon liquid smoke

Make this dish for your Taco Bar (page 237) or BYO Wide-Open Burrito Bowl (page 229) and it will vanish. This spicy addition is a snazzy option on our Open-Faced Chickpea Omelet 3.0 (page 73), or try swapping it into our Barbecue Pulled Portobello Sliders (page 185). If you use tempeh, it will have a firmer texture than tofu when crumbled.

1. Make the chorizo sauce: In a medium bowl, combine the chili powder, garlic powder, cumin, turmeric, oregano, smoked paprika, pepper, vinegar, tamari, and 3 tablespoons water.

2. In a large nonstick pan over medium-high heat, cook the onions. Stir until they are translucent, about 3 minutes, then add the crumbled tempeh or tofu and liquid smoke. Stir until well mixed and the tempeh or tofu becomes slightly browned, lower the heat to medium-low, and add the chorizo sauce. Stir and stir and stir until everything is well coated. If the sauce is sticking to the pan too much, add 1 tablespoon water at a time and decrease the heat to low.

3. The chorizo is ready when most of the sauce has cooked off and the tempeh or tofu is well coated and fragrant, about 5–8 minutes.

APPLE SAGE PAN-FRIED TEMPEH

Heart disease–friendly

MAKES ABOUT 2 CUPS

8 ounces tempeh, cut into ½-inch cubes

3 tablespoons low-sodium tamari

¼ teaspoon liquid smoke or smoked paprika

1 tablespoon applesauce

1 tablespoon maple syrup, optional

1 tablespoon apple cider vinegar

½ teaspoon dried sage

Pinch of ground black pepper

These little flavor bombs have a bit of everything: some heat, some sweet, some salt, and some hidden sage. And they are so easy! Add them to BYO Braw Barley Bowl (page 231), smother them in Mommy's Mushroom Gravy 3.0 (page 87), or serve them with Sweet and Savory Brussels Sprouts (page 190) and baked Yukon Gold potatoes.

1. In a medium bowl, combine the tempeh cubes, tamari, and liquid smoke. Stir until the tempeh cubes are well coated. Set aside.

2. In a small bowl, stir together the applesauce, maple syrup (if using), vinegar, sage, and pepper until well combined.

3. In a large nonstick pan over medium-high heat, pour in the tempeh cubes and any extra liquid, stirring while the tempeh cubes start to brown. As soon as the last of the tamari cooks off, 2 to 3 minutes, remove the pan from the heat and immediately add the applesauce mixture. Stir until well coated. Serve warm, or keep warm over low heat with a close eye on the pan to avoid drying out.

SAVORY TOFU or TEMPEH CUBES

Heart disease–friendly

MAKES ABOUT 2 CUPS

12 ounces firm or extra-firm tofu, pressed (see page 166), or 12 ounces tempeh, cut into ½-inch cubes

3 cloves garlic, minced

¼ cup low-sodium tamari

¼ cup balsamic vinegar (see page 95)

1 teaspoon dried oregano

1 teaspoon crushed dried rosemary

½ teaspoon dried marjoram

We prefer to use the oven when making Savory Tofu Cubes; it makes them firmer and nicely browned on the edges. The tempeh is better pan fried. Both are tasty and versatile. Use the marinade as a salad dressing, too!

1. For tofu, preheat the oven to 400°F and line a sheet pan with parchment paper. For tempeh, you will need a nonstick pan.

2. In a medium bowl, combine the garlic, tamari, vinegar, oregano, rosemary, and marjoram. Add the tofu or tempeh cubes and stir to coat with the marinade. Marinate for at least 10 minutes.

3. For the tofu: Pour the tofu and marinade onto the prepared pan and bake for 20 to 25 minutes, until slightly browned and baked to desired firmness.

4. For the tempeh: Use the stovetop instructions in our Basic Pan-Fried Tempeh Cubes (page 167) recipe.

CHAPTER 9

APPETIZERS, SIDES, and CLEVER EXTRAS

Ann says she doesn't snack because she never knows when the snack is supposed to end! So, she thinks the recipes here should be in the lunch or dinner chapter. She'd eat the whole tray or pan alone—as a "snack"!

We recommend sharing these appetizer recipes with pals interested in becoming Plant-Based Women Warriors. If they take down the whole tray, like Ann, that's perfect—they have found their tribe. Welcome.

GREEN BEANS with SESAME CRUMBLE

Heart disease-friendly

SERVES 2-4

SESAME CRUMBLE

2 tablespoons sesame seeds

2 teaspoons low-sodium tamari

1 teaspoon maple syrup

12 ounces green beans, trimmed

This recipe takes green beans to a whole new level of deliciousness. We always get rave reviews when we serve it, and best of all it is easy to make! You may have a little extra Sesame Crumble, which is good on anything from brown rice to broccoli.

1. Make the Sesame Crumble: In a small pan over medium heat, toast the sesame seeds, stirring until they begin to brown and become fragrant. They brown *easily*, so don't leave them alone. Place the toasted sesame seeds in a coffee grinder (first choice) or a small blender and grind until they just begin to break down and become incredibly fragrant. Careful not to overblend (if that happens, they will still be good but not crumbly). In a small bowl, combine the ground sesame seeds with the tamari and maple syrup.

2. In a medium pot, cover the green beans with water and bring to a boil. Reduce the heat to medium and cook about 6 minutes, or until the beans are tender, then drain.

3. Stir in the Sesame Crumble and serve triumphantly!

CILANTRO-MINT
SAUCE, page 83

CAULIFLOWER FRITTERS

Heart disease-friendly

SERVES 6

1 cup finely diced red onion

½ green finger pepper, minced, seeds removed

1 tablespoon minced fresh ginger

½ cup cilantro, roughly chopped

1½ cups chickpea flour

1 teaspoon turmeric

1 teaspoon Indian red chili powder, or to taste

1 teaspoon garam masala

½ teaspoon ajowan seeds, optional

1 tablespoon lemon juice

¼ teaspoon salt, optional

¼ teaspoon ground black pepper

¼ teaspoon garlic powder

1 medium head cauliflower, cut into florets (6–8 cups)

Just the name of this recipe makes our stomachs growl. Inspiration for this comes from PlantBased IndianLiving.com. The website is a delightful discovery—loaded with delicious, healthy versions of Indian food. Ingredients like finger pepper, a hot pepper used in Indian cuisine; red chili powder (which has a different profile than the chili powder typically used in American cooking); and ajowan seeds are available at grocery stores specializing in Indian or Asian cooking. It is definitely worth the trip!

1. Preheat the oven to 375°F. Line a sheet pan with parchment paper.

2. In a large bowl, combine the red onion, finger pepper, ginger, cilantro, chickpea flour, turmeric, red chili powder, garam masala, ajowan seeds (if using), lemon juice, salt (if using), black pepper, garlic powder, and 1¼ cups water and mix well. Add the cauliflower florets to the batter and coat evenly.

3. Pour the cauliflower onto the prepared pan, placing each floret a little bit apart. Bake for 30 minutes, then flip with a spatula and bake for another 30 minutes, or until the fritters reach your desired level of crispiness.

ROASTED CAULIFLOWER and BROCCOLI BITES

Heart disease–friendly

SERVES 6

1 tablespoon low-sodium tamari

1 teaspoon dried minced onion

1 teaspoon dried granulated garlic

1 teaspoon black sesame seeds

1 teaspoon sesame seeds

½ teaspoon poppy seeds, optional

1 small head cauliflower, broken into bite-size florets

2 broccoli crowns, broken into bite-size florets

2 tablespoons nutritional yeast

Call this a go-to or a "can-do" recipe. It ticks all the boxes: easy to make and pleases the crowd. Throw it on the menu tonight. You'll win.

1. Preheat the oven to 400°F. Line a sheet pan with parchment paper.

2. In a large bowl, combine 1 tablespoon water, the tamari, onion, granulated garlic, black and white sesame seeds, and poppy seeds (if using). Add the cauliflower and broccoli florets and toss until coated with moisture and dotted with spices.

3. Pour the florets onto the prepared pan and spread out evenly. Sprinkle the nutritional yeast over the top and bake for 25 minutes, or until the cauliflower and broccoli tips begin to blacken. Serve warm or cold—either way these are delicious.

TIP:

Use 1 tablespoon of Trader Joe's Everything but the Bagel Sesame Seasoning Blend if you do not have the minced onion, granulated garlic, black sesame seeds, sesame seeds, and poppy seeds.

FLINN'S TIP:

Ann's granddaughter suggests getting a variety of plants in there by adding all kinds of vegetables to the sheet pan for roasting: sliced onion, halved brussels sprouts, cubed summer squash, cubed zucchini, and cherry tomatoes!

BARBECUE PULLED PORTOBELLO SLIDERS with GREEN GODDESS SAUCE

To make heart disease–friendly: Swap out the Green Goddess Sauce for Hummus We Love (page 91) prepared without tahini (or another oil- and tahini-free hummus) or a heart disease–friendly sauce (see pages 76–77, 79–81, 84–87)

SERVES 4

1 tube polenta (sometimes called a "chub" of polenta) or roughly twelve 2½-inch rounds if you make your own polenta

4 large portobello mushroom caps, ideally with stems

½ teaspoon liquid smoke, or to taste

1 cup sliced onion

1–2 cups chiffonade-cut napa cabbage

½ cup barbecue sauce, your favorite, or to taste

½ cup Green Goddess Sauce and Dressing (page 81)

1 cup fresh spinach

Sounds like pulled pork? Yes, we know! And this is as tasty as any barbecue favorite. We serve these up open-faced on rounds of polenta, but the savory mushroom foundation of this recipe highlights any meal. Try it over brown rice, in a sandwich, in a pita, in a BYO Bowl buffet, or just over greens. Our tip: Make extra! Serve this alongside another handsome dish, such as Curried Cauliflower Salad with Lentils and Grapes (page 155), Three Goddesses Salad (page 147), or Roasted Cauliflower and Broccoli Bites (page 183).

1. Preheat the oven to 350°F. Line a sheet pan with parchment paper.

2. Slice the polenta into ⅓-inch-thick rounds. Place the polenta slices onto the prepared pan and bake for 20 minutes, or until warmed throughout.

3. Chop the mushroom caps into cubes or thin strips. If you have stems, pull them apart with your fingers.

4. In a large pan over medium-high heat, cook and stir the mushroom caps and shredded stems in 2 tablespoons water. Once the caps and stems cook down, add ¼ teaspoon of the liquid smoke, stirring it into the mushrooms for a few seconds.

5. Add the onion and napa cabbage, and cook until translucent and tender, 3 to 5 minutes.

6. Reduce the heat to medium-low, and add the barbecue sauce and remaining ¼ teaspoon liquid smoke. Stir well, and taste to see if the overall flavor is right for you. If not, add more barbecue sauce or liquid smoke.

7. To assemble, place the polenta rounds on a platter, and spread a thin layer of Green Goddess Sauce on each round. Top with the spinach leaves, then add a spoonful of the mushrooms. Top with another dollop of Green Goddess Sauce.

SMOKY BARBECUE ZUCCHINI ROUNDS

Heart disease–friendly

SERVES 2–6

1 large zucchini

2 tablespoons barbecue sauce

2–3 tablespoons nutritional yeast

Pinch of smoked paprika

VARIATION:

Out of zucchini? Try using eggplant!

These are easy to make, look delicious, taste fabulous, and are a fun hors d'oeuvre! The key is slicing the zucchini in thin rounds. We like Bone Suckin' barbecue sauce (thick) or Robbie's Hickory Barbeque Sauce, but you can always use your favorite. Most barbecue sauces are not made with added oil, but make sure.

1. Preheat the oven to 400°F. Line a sheet pan with parchment paper.

2. Slice the zucchini about ¼ inch thick, or as thin as possible. The thinner the slices, the crispier they will be.

3. Spread a thin layer of barbecue sauce on the bottom of each zucchini slice and place sauce side down on the prepared pan. It's easiest to just dip the spoon in the sauce and then spread, dip again and spread. This way, you don't get too much.

4. Spread another thin barbecue sauce layer on the top of each slice, and then sprinkle with the nutritional yeast and smoked paprika.

5. Bake for 30 minutes, then check to see if they are beginning to burn. If not, cook a little longer, but watch carefully. They should be crispy-ish and browned.

BUTTERNUT SQUASH HUNKS

Heart disease–friendly

MAKES ROUGHLY 4–5 CUPS

1 butternut squash, cubed into 1-inch hunks (see tip, page 138). Leave the skin on, but remove the seeds.

Leave the skin on—we like to eat the hide! Wrestling the squash to the ground and cubing it into 1-inch hunks is the hardest part—but so worth it! Loaded with fiber, micronutrients, and phytochemicals, these hunky bites pop as part of a BYO Bowl dinner or work as a hearty side dish. We love them plain and fresh out of the oven.

1. Preheat the oven to 400°F. Line a sheet pan with parchment paper.

2. Place the butternut squash hunks onto the prepared pan. Bake for 40 minutes, or until the squash hunks are cooked throughout and a bit blackened on the edges.

Top Ten Toppings *for* Air-Popped Popcorn

Our favorite way to snack on air-popped popcorn is to lightly spray it with Bragg Liquid Aminos Spray or low-sodium tamari, which you may need to transfer to a spray bottle. Toss, then add nutritional yeast and garlic powder, and toss again. The spray not only adds a little saltiness but helps the nutritional yeast to stick. Our friend Lisa surprised us when she told us her favorite way to eat air-popped popcorn is with Bragg Liquid Aminos Spray, nutritional yeast, and several shakes of Frank's Red Hot Sauce. As she says, "Yeaaah, baby!" And we agree. We'd never thought to add hot sauce! This inspired us to ask other plant-based pals about their favorite toppings. Below are the top ten air-popped popcorn party additions:

- Low-sodium tamari
- Bragg Liquid Aminos Spray
- Nutritional yeast
- Hot sauce
- Everything bagel seasoning blend
- Red pepper flakes
- Parsley flakes
- Mix of thyme, oregano, rosemary, and garlic powder
- Vegan chocolate chips and sea salt (chocolate chips are not heart disease–friendly)
- Wasabi powder in the base of the bowl

A BUNCH
OF BS:
THE
BRUSSELS
SPROUTS
SECTION

**BRUSSELS SPROUT
TOTS, page 191**

**BUFFALO
BRUSSELS**

**SWEET *and* SAVORY
BRUSSELS, page 190**

We love filling up on BS! In sixteenth-century Belgium, these little baby cabbages became a favorite. Thus, the French named the popular dish after the city of Brussels's love for the vegetable. We must have genes from that neck of the woods because we love our brussels sprouts any which way. When they are not prepared well, it is a wrestling match to chew or even swallow them. But, when seasoned correctly and cooked throughout, these beloved bombs of vitamin K, vitamin C, fiber, and anticancer compounds are delightful! Here are our favorite ways to prepare brussels sprouts so you, too, can fill up on BS.

BUFFALO BRUSSELS

Heart disease-friendly

We could eat these at every meal, especially in the winter. Best of all, this is such an easy recipe. You are the governor here: If you seek more heat, add more sriracha; if you don't like a lot of heat, use less. We find that a little bit of heat makes these Buffalo Brussels work as hors d'oeuvres, part of a meal, or just right off the sheet pan! We recommend Green Goddess Sauce and Dressing (page 81) or Lemon Tahini Sauce (page 82) for dipping.

SERVES 4

¼ cup nutritional yeast

1 teaspoon hot sauce
(we prefer sriracha)

2 tablespoons balsamic vinegar
(see page 95)

About 20 brussels sprouts, halved

Preheat the oven to 400°F. Line a sheet pan with parchment paper.

In a medium bowl, stir together the nutritional yeast, hot sauce, vinegar, and 3 tablespoons water.

Add the brussels sprouts to the bowl, stir until coated, and then spread on the prepared pan. These will brown with the cut side facing up or down. Bake for 25–30 minutes, or until nicely browned.

SWEET *and* SAVORY BRUSSELS SPROUTS

Heart disease–friendly

This recipe offers your tongue everything it seeks: a little sweet, a little savory (with the umami of tamari), and a little salt. Delicious balance.

SERVES 4

About 20 brussels sprouts, halved

3 tablespoons maple syrup

2 tablespoons low-sodium tamari

1 teaspoon dried onion flakes

1 teaspoon black sesame seeds

½ teaspoon garlic powder

¼ teaspoon ground black pepper

¼ teaspoon salt, optional

Preheat the oven to 400°F. Line a sheet pan with parchment paper.

In a large bowl, combine the brussels sprouts, maple syrup, tamari, onion flakes, black sesame seeds, garlic powder, pepper, and salt (if using). Pour the brussels sprouts and any extra sauce onto the prepared pan. Arrange the brussels sprouts so the flat or cut side is facing down. Bake for 30 minutes, or until the brussels sprouts are browned all over.

TIP:

Use 1 tablespoon of Trader Joe's Everything but the Bagel Sesame Seasoning Blend if you do not have the onion flakes, garlic powder, and black sesame seeds.

BRUSSELS SPROUT TOTS

Heart disease-friendly

This coating transforms brussels sprouts into a tavern-style appetizer—a savory, coated finger food.

SERVES ABOUT 4

8 ounces Hummus We Love (page 91) or any oil-free hummus

2 tablespoons dried oregano

1 tablespoon crushed dried rosemary

2 teaspoons garlic powder

2 teaspoons onion powder

¼ teaspoon turmeric

20–30 brussels sprouts, halved

Preheat the oven to 400°F. Line a sheet pan with parchment paper.

In a large bowl, combine the hummus, oregano, rosemary, garlic powder, onion powder, turmeric, and ½ cup water.

Place the brussels sprouts in the bowl and stir to coat. Pour the brussels sprouts and any extra sauce onto the prepared pan. Separate so they will bake well on all sides.

Bake for 30 to 35 minutes, until tender in the center and browned and a wee bit crispy on the outside.

GET IN A PICKLE

We have found such variety and beauty in pickling veggies. Sometimes we use just vinegar; other times we add a pinch of sweet or salt (or both). A lot of room for experimentation here!

JILLIAN'S QUICK PICKLES

Heart disease-friendly

Our friends Jillian and Chris do things right. They have a huge garden and four green thumbs. They know exactly what will thrive and the right time to plant it, and what they can't eat, they preserve or can. We are so envious! Jillian is also the savvy codirector of my Well, Now! Camp for Plant-Based Women Warriors, which is a total blast. She brings her pickles to camp for burger night and the pickle eating contest. Come join us!

1–1½ cups your favorite fresh vegetables: carrots, radishes, onion, cauliflower, green beans, cucumbers, or beets, whole or sliced

2 cups (roughly) rice vinegar or apple cider vinegar

1–2 tablespoons red wine vinegar

2–3 tablespoons maple syrup

1 teaspoon salt

4 cloves garlic

4 sprigs fresh herbs, such as thyme or rosemary

1 tablespoon black peppercorns

In a 64-ounce jar with a lid, place the vegetables. Add 2 cups water, the rice vinegar, red wine vinegar, maple syrup, salt, garlic, herbs, and peppercorns. The liquid should cover the vegetables in the jar—add more if needed in roughly equal parts vinegar and water. Tightly secure the lid, gently shake it all up, and place in the fridge. Serve as a flavor-filled addition to your brown rice bowls or salads, or just snack on them. They last for weeks in the fridge.

FLINN'S PICKLED CABBAGE

Heart disease-friendly

Flinn is the first grandchild to stride out into the working world—and she's doing it with Flinn style and flair! When we asked her for any recipes, she responded immediately with a half dozen! (See Flinn's Hummus Bowl, page 225.) For this tangy recipe, Flinn suggests using cabbage, but you can experiment with any veggies you love, such as carrots, onion, green beans, cucumbers, or artichoke hearts. We make this in old 32-ounce pasta jars.

½ purple cabbage, shredded (or however much fits)

1 cup (roughly) apple cider vinegar

1 tablespoon maple syrup

1 clove garlic, minced

½ teaspoon salt, optional

¼ teaspoon ground black pepper

In a 32-ounce jar, place as much cabbage as possible. Add the apple cider vinegar, roughly 1 cup water, the maple syrup, garlic, salt (if using), and black pepper. The liquid should cover the vegetables in the jar—add more if needed in roughly equal parts vinegar and water. Tightly secure the lid, gently shake it all up, and place in the fridge. Serve as a crisp addition to your sandwiches, bowls, or salads. It lasts for weeks in the fridge!

PICKLED PURPLE ONION *with* PARSLEY

Heart disease-friendly

The Happy Pear lads got us onto pickling onions. These adorable vegan twins from Ireland, fresh out of the rugby scrum of young adulthood, decided to start a greengrocer in their hometown of Greystones. Their authenticity and energy make them irresistible. They are doing amazing work to get folks to "Eat More Veg!" Warning: It is easy to binge-watch their YouTube channel. They will turn you on to more than just pickling your onions!

Serve these bright, crisp add-ons at all your Build Your Own bowl parties. Add them to sandwiches. Serve along with salsa for a Taco Bar (page 237), with BYO Braw Barley Bowls (page 231), or in BYO Buddha Bowls (page 221).

1 small purple onion, thinly sliced into half-moon strips

½ cup (roughly) rice vinegar

Pinch of salt, optional

3 sprigs parsley, for beauty

In an 8-ounce jar with a lid, place as much of the sliced onion as possible. Fill the jar halfway with rice vinegar and the other half with water. Add a pinch of salt (if using) and your sprigs of parsley. Tightly secure the lid, gently shake it all up, and place in the fridge. It lasts for weeks in the fridge!

LUCKY NUTS

MAKES 2 CUPS

2 cups mixed nuts and seeds, such as walnuts, cashews, pecans, almonds, pistachios, and/or pumpkin seeds

1 tablespoon maple syrup

½ teaspoon curry powder

⅛ teaspoon cayenne pepper

⅛ teaspoon smoked paprika

⅛ teaspoon turmeric

½ teaspoon dried rosemary or 1½ teaspoons minced fresh rosemary

¼ teaspoon salt, optional

Jackie Acho introduced us to these Lucky Nuts at a party, or perhaps more accurately, these nuts introduced us to Jackie. We insisted on meeting the maker of the delicious nuts, and it was our luck indeed, as Jackie continues to be one wise woman warrior in our lives. Whip up these Lucky Nuts for your next gathering and observe the good fortune delivered your way.

1. Preheat the oven to 325°F. Line a sheet pan with parchment paper.

2. In a medium bowl, combine the nuts and seeds. Add the maple syrup, curry powder, cayenne pepper, smoked paprika, turmeric, rosemary, and salt (if using) and toss to combine. Transfer the coated nuts to the prepared pan and spread evenly in one layer. Bake 15 to 20 minutes, until the nuts are fragrant and lightly toasted.

SEED and NUT BARK

2 cups raw pumpkin seeds

1½ cups raw pecans

¾ cup raw sunflower seeds

¼ cup slivered almonds

2 tablespoons flaxseed meal

2 tablespoons chia seeds

3–4 tablespoons maple syrup

Running out of ingredients is sometimes the best! One day, we wanted to make seed bark from *The Engine 2 Cookbook*, yet we realized we did not have all the ingredients. So, we jazzed together a combination of what we did have and discovered a new favorite! This is the perfect dish to take to a party, serve as an appetizer, or carry as a snack.

1. Preheat the oven to 350°F. Line a sheet pan with parchment paper.

2. In a medium bowl, combine the pumpkin seeds, pecans, sunflower seeds, almonds, flaxseed meal, chia seeds, and maple syrup.

3. Toss all the ingredients until well coated. Transfer the mixture to the prepared pan and press into a layer about ¼ inch thick. Bake for 18 minutes, rotating the pan halfway through if your oven bakes unevenly. Do not let it burn.

4. Remove from the oven and let cool for 10 minutes—you will hear the bark crackling as it cools. This is an important stage as this is when it stiffens and gets crunchy. Then, break the bark into chunks and serve. Store extra in an airtight container when completely cooled.

CHAPTER 10

CRACKERS, QUICK BREADS, and OTHER FILLERS

How to start a meal? Want to fill out other dishes? Or just stretch mealtime a bit longer? This section is comfort—filling in the cracks and topping off the tank. Dinner for the whole gang? Home alone on a rainy day? Or on the go? Here you go.

SEED and MILLET CRACKERS

Heart disease–friendly

**MAKES ROUGHLY
120 CRACKERS,
DEPENDING ON
DESIRED SIZE**

2 cups old-fashioned rolled oats

1 cup millet flour or chickpea flour

½ cup sunflower seeds

½ cup sesame seeds

2 tablespoons flaxseed meal

½ cup black sesame seeds, optional

1 tablespoon dried minced onion or onion flakes

1 tablespoon garlic granules or garlic powder

¼ teaspoon salt, optional

TIP:
If you find your cupboard is missing the minced onion, garlic granules, and black sesame seed for this recipe, you can hack that problem by using a few tablespoons (to taste) of Trader Joe's Everything but the Bagel Sesame Seasoning Blend or another everything bagel seasoning.

If you cannot find millet flour, use chickpea flour! When we first made these crackers, we sat at home watching the rain and snow outside. The house smelled divinely of fresh crackers, and we ate the whole batch. Add the black sesame seeds for a great pop of contrast color and flavor.

1. Preheat the oven to 350°F. Line two sheet pans with parchment paper.

2. In a large bowl, combine the oats, millet flour, sunflower seeds, sesame seeds, flaxseed meal, black sesame seeds, dried onion, garlic granules, and salt (if using) until well mixed. Add 2½ cups water and stir until well combined. It should be the texture of lumpy, uncooked oatmeal. If it's too thick, add more water (up to ½ cup). Allow the mixture to sit for a few minutes and thicken.

3. Pour the mixture evenly onto the prepared pans and smooth it into an even layer no more than ¼ inch thick.

4. Set the sheet pans in the oven and bake for 15 minutes.

5. After 15 minutes, remove from the oven and cut into desired cracker size with a pizza cutter—we cut roughly 1½ × 1½-inch squares. Bake for 40 more minutes. Turn off the oven and let the crackers remain in the oven for 10 more minutes with the door open. Taste a cracker to see if it's crispy throughout. If not, leave in the warm oven for 10 minutes more with the oven door closed. Rotate the pans if you find the top pan or lower pan is browning more than the other. Taste again for crispness.

6. If they still need to be crispier, cycle through the following 10-minute stages: 10 minutes in the oven at 350°F, 10 minutes with the oven off and door open, and 10 minutes in the oven with the door closed, tasting after each stage.

7. Allow the crackers to cool completely, then serve with Balsamic Hummus (page 91), Hickory Smokehouse Hummus (page 92), or Hummus We Love (page 91); prepare the hummus without tahini to make heart disease–friendly. Store in an airtight container for up to 2 weeks.

QUICK and EASY BEER BREAD

Heart disease–friendly

**MAKES ONE
8½ × 4½-INCH LOAF**

2 cups spelt or white whole wheat flour

1 cup old-fashioned rolled oats, plus more for dusting

1 teaspoon baking powder

1 tablespoon maple syrup

One 12-ounce can beer or seltzer water

1 tablespoon balsamic vinegar (white or light colored recommended; see page 95)

Nutritional yeast, for dusting

At one of Ann's presentations, a woman once approached her excited to share her daughter's recipe for beer bread. She called her daughter on the spot and got it from her over the phone! Ann knew it was a keeper when two of her granddaughters reached for seconds. Both spelt flour and white whole wheat flour (a bit lighter than whole wheat but every bit as healthy) work well. For a wheat-free version, you can use oat flour, but the bread will be denser and heavier. Parchment paper helps the bread release easily from the pan. Ann says it's heavenly to toast this bread and eat with fresh fruit or a good jam on each bite.

1. Preheat the oven to 350°F. Line an 8½ × 4½-inch loaf pan with parchment paper or use a nonstick loaf pan.

2. In a large bowl, mix together the flour, oats, baking powder, maple syrup, and beer. The mixture will be sticky. Add to the loaf pan and spread out evenly.

3. Spread the balsamic vinegar on the top, then sprinkle with nutritional yeast and a dusting of oats.

4. Bake for 60 minutes, or until the top is browned and the center of the bread is thoroughly cooked. It is done when a toothpick or thin knife blade comes out of the center of the loaf clean. If you didn't use parchment paper, loosen with a knife around the sides. Wait 5 to 10 minutes and the bread should come out easily (hopefully).

JANE'S TALL
FLAX BISCUITS

ANN'S SHORT
FLAX BISCUITS,
page 208

JANE'S TALL FLAX BISCUITS

MAKES 8–10, DEPENDING ON THE SIZE

½ cup walnut pieces

2 cups whole wheat flour or oat flour, plus more as needed

3 tablespoons flaxseed meal

1 teaspoon baking soda

½ teaspoon baking powder

¼ teaspoon salt, optional

1 cup oat milk or your favorite nondairy milk

Eat these HOT! They are filled with such goodness, fiber, and flax. Smother them with jam, dip them into New Senate Soup (page 135), pair them with our Wonder Woman Salad (page 149), or dunk them in Mommy's Mushroom Gravy 3.0 (page 87). Warning: It is easy to eat half of these without blinking!

1. Preheat the oven to 400°F. Line a sheet pan with parchment paper.

2. In a food processor, combine the walnuts and 2 tablespoons water until a paste forms. Add the whole wheat flour, flaxseed meal, baking soda, baking powder, and salt (if using) and carefully pulse 8 to 10 times, until everything mixes into a crumble with a mealy texture. Add the oat milk and pulse 8 to 10 more times, until the flour is incorporated and a dough forms. (It should be the texture of biscuit dough.) If it is too wet, add a few tablespoons of flour and gently pulse again (we usually have to add a few tablespoons when using oat flour but not as much with whole wheat).

3. Lightly dust the prepared pan with flour and place the dough onto the dusted area of the pan. Gently press the dough with your fingertips so it is roughly ½ inch high. Using a 2-inch-wide drinking glass or biscuit cutter, cut out biscuits and arrange them on the pan. Combine the remaining dough bits and pieces into biscuits—these imperfect edge-y ones are our favorite. Bake for 12 to 13 minutes, until lightly browned and cooked throughout the center. These Tall Flax Biscuits are always best served hot and fresh!

ANN'S SHORT FLAX BISCUITS

Heart disease-friendly

MAKE 8–10

1 cup oat flour or whole-grain flour of choice

2 tablespoons flaxseed meal or chia seeds

1 teaspoon baking powder

⅔ cup oat milk or other nondairy milk

Jane's Tall Flax Biscuits (page 207) were the impetus for this recipe, but we make these without walnuts and a few other ingredients. They aren't nearly as tall as Jane's—but lower and flatter, like a pancake or a cookie. No matter what we call them, they are SO GOOD and perfect for when you just need a fast, delicious, clever addition to a meal. Gobble them up HOT with jam, fruit, or with our Carrot Mushroom Red Lentil Soup (page 141). If you have any the next day, try toasting them until they are crispy—so good!

1. Preheat the oven to 400°F. Line a sheet pan with parchment paper.

2. In a small bowl, mix together the oat flour, flaxseed meal, and baking powder.

3. Add the oat milk and stir briefly until just mixed. Don't over-mix. The mixture has to be lumpy and maybe even have some streaks of flour—otherwise the biscuits turn out tough.

4. Pour or scoop 8 to 10 heaping tablespoons of the mixture onto the prepared pan. Gently flatten the tops a little bit if you choose. Bake for 14 minutes, or until lightly brown on top. These do not rise like biscuits but, as noted, are flat like pancakes or cookies.

NAAN BREAD

Heart disease-friendly

MAKES 6 NAAN

¾ cup almond milk, oat milk, soy milk, or water, warmed to around 100°F (bath temperature)

2¼ teaspoons active dry yeast

1 tablespoon maple syrup

1 cup whole wheat flour, plus about ¼ cup for dusting

½ cup chickpea flour

½ teaspoon baking powder

¼ teaspoon salt, optional

4 cloves garlic, minced

2 tablespoons chopped cilantro

Indian food from PlantBasedIndianLiving.com inspired us to get cooking with more flavor, confidence, and Indian spice. One of our first dishes was naan bread—not so risky, a blast to learn, and a boost to our confidence. As we do with so many dishes, we have made a few tweaks to the original recipe. Please visit their website for more notes and inspiration on cooking delicious Indian food.

1. In a small bowl, mix together the warmed almond milk, yeast, and maple syrup. Set aside for at least 10 minutes to let the yeast activate. The yeast mixture will have bubbles on the surface, which is a sign the yeast is doing its thing!

2. In a large bowl, combine the whole wheat flour, chickpea flour, baking powder, and salt (if using) and mix.

3. Pour the yeast mixture into the flour mixture and mix well. Continue mixing and kneading until a dough ball forms. If the dough is sticky, dust with an additional tablespoon or so of flour and continue kneading.

4. Cover the bowl with a damp cloth, set aside, and allow to rise for at least 10 minutes at room temperature.

5. Remove the dough from the bowl and transfer to a floured work surface. Knead the dough until it's no longer sticky and any air pockets are gone.

6. Divide the dough into six roughly equal pieces and roll each into a ball. Slightly flatten the balls into 3-inch-diameter pucks. Set aside.

7. Heat a nonstick pan over medium heat.

8. On a flour-dusted surface, with a rolling pin, roll one dough ball at a time into an oval or circle. Flip and dust again, if needed, after every roll to avoid sticking to the surface. Consider rolling out all the dough balls before cooking—otherwise your eye is off the cooking naan.

recipe continues

9. Using your hand or a basting brush, apply a thin layer of water to one side of the rolled naan dough.

10. Place the wet side of the naan dough on the heated pan. Lightly press a small portion of garlic and cilantro into the top surface of the dough. Once you see big bubbles on the surface, it is time to flip the naan. (Bubbles are a good sign—they mean the bread is cooking from the inside, too.) You'll see the surface is nicely browned and blackened in areas. Cook evenly on both sides. Serve warm.

CLAVA CAIRN SODA BREAD

Heart disease–friendly

SERVES 4

1½ cups whole wheat flour or oat flour or a mix of your choosing, plus 2 tablespoons (if needed) for shaping and dusting

1 tablespoon flaxseed meal

½ teaspoon baking soda

½ teaspoon baking powder

¼ teaspoon sea salt, optional

¾ cup oat milk or other nondairy milk

1 tablespoon apple cider vinegar

A visit to the Clava Cairns in Scotland and its solstice-light-seeking domes inspired the shape of this soda bread. It is said the slim passage to the center of the curious stone structures channels a burst of light only on the winter solstice. What a moment, what ancient knowledge. Ancient Scots also used rising agents and acid—traditionally sour milk (eek!)—in their soda bread. According to lore, they marked the top of their soda bread with an *X* to protect the household and let the fairies out. While we use apple cider vinegar instead of sour milk, we shape the loaf like a Clava Cairn mound with a channel to the center, and we also score an *X* on top so the fairies can escape.

1. Preheat the oven to 400°F. Line a sheet pan with parchment paper.

2. In a large bowl, combine the flour, flaxseed meal, baking soda, baking powder, salt (if using), oat milk, and apple cider vinegar. Place the dough on the sheet pan and shape it with your hands into a mound (about softball size). Sprinkle another tablespoon or so of flour on the mound if the dough is sticky. It is not like typical bread dough—it has a more soupy and sticky texture. Don't forget to mark the top of the loaf with an *X* or re-create a wee Clava Cairn shape as we like to do. Or do both!

3. Bake immediately for 23 to 28 minutes, until browned on top. Serve warm with soup or jam or plain.

CHAPTER 11

BUILD YOUR OWN BOWLS, HANDHELD MEALS, and DINNER FEASTS

The word *pelvis* means "basin" or "bowl." Symbolically, what is more womanly and powerful than the pelvis? What it creates. What it holds. Family, life, pleasure—vitality!

continues

Now, build your own bowl for dinner, for what's in your bowl builds you. Be unique. We are fortified by how we personally fill, layer, drizzle, dollop, and garnish our own bowls. The aim is for each bite to taste unique. When building your own bowl, one rule stands: Each bowl starts with a bed of greens—cooked kale, steamed greens, fresh spinach, spring mix, baby arugula—any greens will do.

When you are having dinner outside or on the go, sometimes a handheld option seems more suitable. Again, don't forget to find a way to get the greens on that burger or with those nuggets!

Other times, dinner is a cozy gathering and the smell of a dish cooking has filled your home and lured everyone to the table—we love those one-dish dinners as well. Truth be told, we usually have a Warrior Salad (see chapter 7) alongside the astounding Chickpea Masala (page 245), Ann's Open-Faced Twice-Baked Potatoes (page 263), or Sweet Potato and Cashew Ricotta Lasagna (page 259).

BUILD
YOUR OWN
BOWLS

Without a lesson plan, Ann taught us all the beauty of personalizing our one-bowl meals. She always piles the lazy Susan table high at dinnertime with tempting options. So, it is a riot to hear Ann declare, "I do not make bowls. I prepare 'one main thing.'" Well, that "one main thing" may be brown rice and black beans with salsa, thawed frozen corn, a heap of spring greens, some chopped tomatoes, maybe a diced red pepper, and a few green onions. Then, the lazy Susan starts to spin as we build our own bowls. The following recipes are our favorite combinations, but have fun getting creative yourself!

FORBIDDEN BOWL

To make heart disease-friendly: Use a heart disease-friendly sauce (see pages 76–77, 79–81, 84–87) and leave out the avocado

When we discovered black rice, we thought we'd hit gold. When we learned it had another secret name, *forbidden rice*, it became even cooler. Then, we tried black rice noodles and forbidden rice noodles—shut the front door! We were hooked. We could not wait to invent a Forbidden Bowl filled with superfoods we love. And without fail, each time we make it, we change up the sauce or add another vegetable or fruit. Once, we even added blueberries. We recommend any of our sauces with the Forbidden Bowl. The ones we use most are our Sesame Ginger Sauce (page 80) and our Lightning Dressing (page 101).

SERVES 3–4

Teriyaki Tofu or Tempeh Cubes (page 169)

10 ounces black rice noodles or 1–2 cups black rice

4–6 cups greens (we prefer thinly sliced napa cabbage, chopped bok choy, or fresh spring greens)

1 large sweet potato, cooked and cubed (see page 48)

1½ cups shelled edamame, thawed

½ cup grated or sliced carrot

1 mango, cubed

¼ purple cabbage, sliced

3 green onions, finely chopped

1 avocado, cubed, optional

Sauce of your choice (we prefer Sesame Ginger Sauce, page 80, or Lightning Dressing, page 101)

Broccoli sprouts, for garnish

Prepare the tofu cubes according to the recipe. Set aside.

Cook the black rice noodles or black rice according to the package directions. Cool the noodles under running water to prevent them from cooking further and sticking together.

Place the greens in a serving bowl next to the noodles. Then create a buffet or tabletop with separate bowls containing the prepared tofu cubes, sweet potato cubes, edamame, carrot, mango, purple cabbage, green onions, avocado (if using), sauce, and sprouts.

Each person then builds their own bowl starting with a bed of greens, adding noodles and other toppings and the finishing touch of sauce and sprouts.

BUDDHA BOWL

To make heart disease–friendly: Use a heart disease–friendly sauce (see pages 76-77, 79-81, 84-87) and leave out the avocado

A Buddha Bowl is the original bowl of all bowls. Our version will fill you with nourishment, balance, and amazing sauce!

SERVES 3-4

Basic Baked Tofu Cubes (page 167) or Basic Pan-Fried Tempeh Cubes (page 167)

1–2 cups brown rice

4–6 cups greens (we prefer fresh spring greens)

1 large sweet potato, cooked and cubed (see page 48)

15 ounces (1½ cups) canned chickpeas, drained and rinsed

2 cups cooked kale (see page 49)

Pickled Purple Onion with Parsley (page 195)

½ cup grated or sliced carrot

3 green onions, finely chopped

1 avocado, cubed, optional

Sauce of your choice (we prefer Lemon Tahini Sauce, page 82)

Broccoli sprouts, for garnish

Prepare the tofu cubes according to the recipe. Set aside.

Cook the brown rice according to the package directions.

Place the greens in a serving bowl next to the brown rice. Then create a buffet or tabletop with separate bowls containing the prepared tofu cubes, sweet potato, chickpeas, kale, Pickled Purple Onion, carrot, green onions, avocado (if using), sauce, and sprouts.

Each person then builds their own bowl starting with a bed of greens, adding brown rice and other toppings and the finishing touch of sauce and sprouts.

ROOTS *and* SHOOTS BOWL

To make heart disease-friendly: Use a heart disease-friendly sauce (see pages 76–77, 79–81, 84–87)

My husband and I met working at Outward Bound—an outdoor leadership and expeditionary school filled with climbing, paddling, and hiking challenges. At the end of each day we debriefed with our crew of students. One of our favorite debriefs was "Roots and Shoots"—as this directed each student to share how they felt grounded as well as where they felt they could grow. Like a good debrief, we find this Roots and Shoots Bowl is grounding and hopeful. On the foundation of tubers and roots, there is a lot of color and flavor.

SERVES 3–4

Teriyaki Tofu or Tempeh Cubes (page 169)

4–6 cups greens (we prefer fresh spring greens)

2 sweet potatoes, cooked and sliced (see page 48)

2 Yukon Gold potatoes, cooked and sliced (see page 49)

2 parsnips, boiled until cooked yet still firm and sliced

2–3 large carrots, boiled until cooked yet still firm and sliced

1 mango, cubed

1 red bell pepper, diced

Thai Peanut Sauce (page 77) or Lemon Tahini Sauce (page 82)

3 green onions, diced

¼ cup cilantro, roughly chopped

¼ cup sprouts or microgreens, for garnish

Prepare the tofu cubes according to the recipe. Set aside.

Place the greens in a serving bowl next to the sliced sweet potatoes, potatoes, parsnips, and carrots. Then create a buffet or tabletop with separate bowls containing the mango, red pepper, sauce, green onions, cilantro, and sprouts.

Each person then builds their own bowl starting with a bed of greens, adding sweet potatoes, potatoes, parsnips, and carrots and other toppings and the finishing touch of sauce, green onions, cilantro, and sprouts.

FLINN'S HUMMUS BOWL

To make heart disease–friendly: Use Lemon or Balsamic Hummus prepared without tahini (page 91) or another oil- and tahini-free hummus

Flinn, a savvy twentysomething and Ann's oldest grandchild, figured out how to whip together a delicious bowl with many components already prepared! Flinn says to cook the rice and roast the veggies while folding laundry, paying bills, and watching Netflix. Then, throw arugula, rice, and the roasted veggies in a bowl and stir, stir, stir in your favorite hummus. Top with pickled whatever you have and some sprouts. You can use any greens for this recipe, but Flinn prefers arugula. Thanks, Flinn!

SERVES 3–4

1–2 cups brown rice

4–6 cups greens (Flinn prefers arugula)

Roasted Cauliflower and Broccoli Bites, following Flinn's Tip (page 183)

Lemon Hummus (page 91), Balsamic Hummus (page 91), or your favorite hummus

Flinn's Pickled Cabbage (page 194)

¼ cup sprouts or microgreens, for garnish

Cook the brown rice according to the package directions.

Place the greens in a serving bowl next to the brown rice. Then create a buffet or tabletop with the Roasted Cauliflower and Broccoli Bites, Lemon Hummus, Flinn's Pickled Cabbage, and sprouts.

Each person then builds their own bowl starting with a bed of arugula, rice, cauliflower, and broccoli, and the finishing touch of hummus, pickled cabbage, and sprouts.

BALANCED RICE NOODLE BOWL

To make heart-disease friendly: Use the Teriyaki Sauce (page 76)

We eat plain brown rice noodles right out of the pot—we love them that much. It is time to stop eating and share them with others when they start to cool to the point that they stick to your fingers! The beauty and balance in our Rice Noodle Bowl always wins over any not-yet-plant-based guests.

SERVES 3–4

Sesame Ginger–Topped Tofu or Tempeh (page 171)

12 ounces brown rice noodles (we prefer Lotus Foods Brown Pad Thai Rice Noodles)

4–6 cups greens (we prefer fresh spring greens)

1 cup shelled edamame, thawed

1½ cups broccoli, steamed

Thai Peanut Sauce (page 77), Teriyaki Sauce (page 76), or Spicy Almond Sauce (page 78)

½ cup cilantro, roughly chopped

¼ cup sprouts or microgreens, for garnish

Prepare the tofu according to the recipe. Set aside.

Cook the brown rice noodles according to the package directions. Cool under running water to prevent them from cooking further and sticking together.

Place the greens in a serving bowl next to the noodles. Then create a buffet or tabletop with separate bowls containing tofu, edamame, steamed broccoli, sauce, cilantro, and sprouts.

Each person then builds their own bowl starting with a bed of greens, adding brown rice noodles and other toppings and the finishing touch of sauce, cilantro, and sprouts.

WIDE-OPEN BURRITO BOWL

To make heart disease–friendly: Leave out the guacamole

It is great fun to pile up your own burrito with all your favorite fillings and toppings! The aim is to pile it so high you can't close it. Sometimes we even leave out the tortilla and just create our beloved bowl of brown rice and black beans.

SERVES 3–4

Chorizo Tempeh or Tofu (page 172), optional

1–2 cups brown rice

4–6 cups greens (we prefer chopped romaine or spring greens)

4 whole-grain or corn tortillas

15 ounces no-fat vegetarian refried beans, warmed

15 ounces canned black beans, drained, rinsed, and warmed

1–2 tomatoes, diced

1–2 red, orange, or green bell peppers, diced

2–3 green onions, diced

Tangy Lime and Sweet Corn Sauce (page 79)

Vibrant Mango Salsa (page 105), or salsa of choice

#1 Guacamole (page 107)

½ cup broccoli sprouts

1 lime, cut into wedges

Prepare the tempeh or tofu according to the recipe (if using). Set aside.

Cook the brown rice according to the package directions.

Place the greens in a serving bowl with the tortillas next to it. Then create a buffet or tabletop with separate bowls containing brown rice, refried beans, black beans, tempeh, tomatoes, peppers, green onions, sauce, salsa, guacamole, broccoli sprouts, and lime wedges.

Each person then builds their own bowl starting with a bed of greens, placing the tortilla on top and adding other toppings and the finishing touch of sauce, salsa, guac, sprouts, and a wedge of lime.

BRAW BARLEY BOWL

To make heart disease–friendly: Use a heart disease–friendly sauce (see pages 76–77, 79–81, 84–87)

Braw is Scottish for "pleasant," and this is one pleasing bowl. Build your own barley-based bowl and tuck in after conquering the peaks of Sgùrr Dearg and Ladhar Bheinn. Or for an afternoon of getting lost in a *stramash* of Highlanders while reading the newest Outlander novel. *Slaite Mhath!*

SERVES 3–4

Apple Sage Pan-Fried Tempeh (page 173), optional

1–2 cups barley

4–6 cups greens (we prefer fresh spring greens)

Cooked Onions, Garlic, and Mushrooms (page 51)

15 ounces canned cannellini beans, drained, rinsed, and warmed

Flinn's Pickled Cabbage (page 194)

Walnut Ginger Sauce and Dressing (page 76) or Walnut Pesto (page 88)

½ cup broccoli sprouts, for garnish

Prepare the tempeh according to the recipe (if using). Set aside.

Cook the barley according to the package directions.

Place the greens in a serving bowl next to the barley. Then create a buffet or tabletop with separate bowls containing the tempeh; cooked onions, garlic, and mushrooms; beans; pickled cabbage; sauce; and broccoli sprouts.

GROOVE-ON QUINOA BOWL

To make heart disease–friendly: Use a heart disease–friendly sauce (see pages 76–77, 79–81, 84–87) and leave out the avocado

Quinoa at every meal sounds like bliss. When cooked until fluffy and the wee ring of the endosperm separates from the grain, it is dreamy. So, if you are like us and could groove through a whole day eating quinoa, try this bowl chock-full of flavor, spice, and sauces galore!

SERVES 3–4

Savory Tofu or Tempeh Cubes (page 175) or Sesame Ginger–Topped Tofu or Tempeh (page 171)

1–2 cups red quinoa, rinsed

4–6 cups greens (we prefer chopped romaine or fresh spring greens)

15 ounces canned black beans (or beans of choice), drained, rinsed, and warmed

2 cups chopped bok choy

1 mango, cubed

1–2 avocados, diced

Green Goddess Sauce and Dressing (page 81), Cashew Pesto (page 89), or sauce of choice

½ cup broccoli sprouts, for garnish

Prepare the tofu according to the recipe. Set aside.

Cook the quinoa according to the package directions.

Place the greens in a serving bowl next to the quinoa. Then create a buffet or tabletop with separate bowls containing the tofu, beans, bok choy, mango, avocado, sauce, and broccoli sprouts.

Each person then builds their own bowl starting with a bed of greens, adding quinoa and other toppings of choice and the finishing touch of sauce and sprouts.

PASTA TONIGHT BOWL

To make heart disease-friendly: Leave out the Avocado Pesto

Pasta, sauce, and veggies—this bowl is a classic—a good old pasta dinner where everyone serves themselves a bowl! Pasta Tonight Bowl scores high with our family as it is fun and familiar to everyone. Here, we have added a twist to the typical "pasta night" with roasted veggies and a few different sauce options. There is no way to lose with this bowl!

SERVES 3-4

1 pound whole-grain pasta

4-6 cups greens (we prefer baby spinach or fresh spring greens)

Roasted Cauliflower and Broccoli Bites (page 183)

Original Marinara (page 84) or Boyfriend Bolognese Sauce (page 85)

Avocado Pesto (page 88), optional

½ cup fresh basil leaves, for garnish

Cook the pasta according to the package directions.

Place the greens in a serving bowl next to the pasta. Then create a buffet or tabletop with the tray of Roasted Cauliflower and Broccoli Bites, sauces of choice, and fresh basil.

Each person then builds their own bowl starting with a bed of greens, adding pasta, veggies, sauces, and a finishing touch of basil.

TACO BAR

To make heart disease-friendly: Leave out the avocado

SERVES 6

12 soft corn tortillas and/or 2 heads romaine lettuce separated into individual spears

3 cups cooked brown rice or cooked quinoa

2 cups canned black beans or brown lentils, drained, rinsed, and warmed

2 large sweet potatoes, roasted and diced (see page 48)

Chorizo Tempeh or Tofu (page 172), optional

Brian's Fresh Salsa, (page 104) or your favorite salsa

Vibrant Mango Salsa (page 105) or cubed mango

1 head romaine lettuce, chopped in ribbons

1 red bell pepper, diced

2 carrots, shredded

2 avocados, sliced or mashed, optional

Hot sauce, your favorite

Rose, Ann's granddaughter (Jane's niece), inspired this beautiful recipe. It is as smart, colorful, and refreshing as Rose! Enjoy it with any and ALL sauces, salsas, or toppings that blow your dress up! It can be messy, and honestly, we spend most of dinner eating the goodies that fall out of our overstuffed romaine leaves or soft tacos! But that's half the fun. Midfeast, take the poll, "Do you rotate your head to the taco or do you rotate the taco to your head?" This recipe serves hungry people or sets you up with delicious leftovers. For an eyebrow-raising, boho twist on taco toppings, Rose recommends serving this with Thai Peanut Sauce (page 77). Sounds equal parts delicious and suspicious!

1. On the table or counter, construct the Taco Bar by placing the components in order. We prefer to build tacos the following way: place tortillas or romaine spears on your plate, add brown rice to the center of each, place beans, sweet potatoes, and tempeh or tofu (if using) in the center of the rice, then from underneath, grab the soft taco in a "taco hold." This settles the rice and beans and raises the walls, which allows one to add the other toppings neatly.

2. Add any or all of the salsas, shredded romaine, pepper, carrots, avocado (if using), and a kiss of hot sauce.

WOMAN WARRIOR BURGERS

To make heart disease-friendly: Leave out the guacamole

MAKES 8–10

2 medium sweet potatoes, cooked and diced (about 1½ cups; see page 48)

1½ cups cooked quinoa

15 ounces canned black beans, drained and rinsed

½ cup diced yellow onion

1 clove garlic, minced

3 tablespoons old-fashioned rolled oats, or more as needed

1 tablespoon maple syrup

2 teaspoons cumin, or to taste

2 teaspoons smoked paprika, or to taste

1 teaspoon coriander

1 teaspoon chili powder

1 teaspoon onion powder

1 teaspoon garlic powder

1 teaspoon dried oregano

¼ cup barbecue sauce, your favorite, for glazing while cooking, optional

8 whole wheat buns, optional (see note)

Women Warriors, make this a *sexy burger*. Go topless and bottomless with no bun! We often serve these on butter lettuce, not to avoid the bread or wheat, but because it is difficult to find 100% whole-wheat buns free of oil and white flour (see note for our favorite brand).

Brenda, Darlene, and Lacey are the Women Warriors of the Plant-Strong Immersion's culinary team. They use the simple foundation of quinoa, sweet potato, and beans for this burger, with added oats and spice for depth and flavor. You can use any kind of quinoa for this recipe—blond, tricolor, or red—and you can sub in white beans or chickpeas for the black beans.

1. Preheat the oven to 400°F. Line a sheet pan with parchment paper.

2. In a large bowl, mash the cooked sweet potatoes. They should be only slightly chunky. Add the cooked quinoa and beans and mash it all together until about half the beans are partly mashed and half are whole. This gives the burgers an amazing texture.

3. In a large pan over medium-high heat, add the onions and cook, while stirring, until fragrant and translucent, about 4 minutes. Add the garlic and stir for another minute or two, until the garlic is fragrant as well.

4. Add the onions and garlic to the burger mixture, along with the oats, maple syrup, cumin, smoked paprika, coriander, chili powder, onion powder, garlic powder, and oregano. Using a spatula or your hands, fold and incorporate the ingredients. Use your hands to form 8 to 10 burger patties, about ⅓ cup each.

5. Place the burger patties on the prepared pan and bake for 20 to 25 minutes. Carefully flip and add a thin layer of barbecue sauce (if using) on top of each burger, then bake another 10 to 20 minutes. (The whole kitchen will smell delicious.)

Optional fixin's: lettuce, tomato, Pickled Purple Onion with Parsley (page 195), ketchup, mustard, relish, #1 Guacamole (page 107)

6. You may need to adjust oven times depending on the burger size, thickness, and whether your stove is electric or gas . . . just be attentive!

7. Serve with buns (if using) and fixin's. Or go ahead and make that topless and bottomless sexy burger.

NOTE:

If you'd like to enjoy these on a bun, we recommend sprouted whole-grain, no-oil buns from the Food for Life Ezekiel 4:9 product line.

BEAN BURGER IN A FLASH

WOMAN WARRIOR BURGER, page 238

BEAN BURGERS IN A FLASH

Heart disease–friendly

MAKES 5

15 ounces canned no-salt black beans (about 1½ cups), drained and rinsed

1 medium onion, chopped (about 1 cup)

½ cup old-fashioned rolled oats, plus more as needed

1 tablespoon chili powder

½ teaspoon turmeric

2 tablespoons flaxseed meal

3 tablespoons salsa, plus more as needed

1 cup cooked and chopped greens, optional (about 2 cups uncooked)

Amazing how much these look like hamburgers, but they taste 100 percent better! They hold together well and best of all they are easy and fast to make—with ingredients at the ready, six minutes! We first had them when we were out of everything except oats and black beans, and they hit the spot. Add other ingredients if you choose: Make them deliciously green with cooked kale, spinach, or collards, or add color with shredded carrots. Be sure to use a chunky salsa.

1. In a large bowl, place the beans, onion, oats, chili powder, turmeric, flaxseed meal, salsa, and cooked greens (if using; be sure to squeeze out the extra water from the greens).

2. Mix and squish the ingredients with your hands. This is our favorite way to prepare these burgers as there is nothing to wash except your hands.

3. The mixture should be moist but not wet. Add more salsa if it is too dry and more oats if it is too wet.

4. Shape into patties with your hands, place directly into a pan or on a plate, and allow to stand for a few minutes. They will hold together better if you can wait.

5. In a large nonstick pan over medium heat, cook the patties for 5 minutes without turning, until browned. With a spatula, carefully flip the burgers and cook another 3 to 4 minutes, until firm and brown.

6. Eat them on their own with ketchup and mustard, barbecue sauce, or more salsa. Or enjoy them on a whole-grain bun (see note, page 239) or bread with all the fixings. You can't miss however you eat these burgers! Freeze extras, but be sure to cook them first.

CRISPY CHECKIN' NUGGETS

Heart disease–friendly

MAKE ROUGHLY 15–20, DEPENDING ON SIZE

15 ounces canned chickpeas (about 1½ cups), aquafaba (bean water) reserved

½ cup diced onion

1 teaspoon garlic, minced

½ cup old-fashioned rolled oats

1 tablespoon nutritional yeast

1 teaspoon smoked paprika

1 teaspoon onion powder

1 tablespoon flaxseed meal

1 tablespoon mustard, your favorite

1 tablespoon low-sodium tamari

¾ cup whole-wheat breadcrumbs, cornflake crumbs, or panko (we prefer Ian's Gluten-Free Panko)

Ketchup or Green Goddess Sauce and Dressing (page 81), for dipping

These crispy nuggets look, smell, and taste just like you hope they will. Crisp and delish! Everyone will peek over your shoulder "checkin' out" what is on your plate. Jane likes these straight-up dipped in ketchup, but Ann finds the plain crispiness satisfying. No matter what shapes you make—nuggets, patties, rounds, or triangles—these brown up nice and crisp. More time in the oven means more crispiness. Aquafaba is what makes the coating, so don't forget to save it when draining the chickpeas!

Serve this fun meal along with an equally playful salad, such as Bright Quinoa Lime Mint Salad (page 153) or Orange Mango Bean Salad (page 157).

1. Preheat the oven to 375°F. Line a sheet pan with parchment paper.

2. In a food processor or high-speed blender, place the chickpeas, onion, garlic, oats, nutritional yeast, smoked paprika, onion powder, flaxseed meal, mustard, and tamari and blend until well mixed, scraping down the sides of the processor as needed.

3. Set up your counter space so the chickpea mixture, bowl of reserved aquafaba, bowl or plate of breadcrumbs, and prepared pan are lined up.

4. Using your hands, shape roughly 1½ tablespoons of chickpea mixture into a nugget shape, coat it with aquafaba, toss it in breadcrumbs, and place on the pan. Repeat until you have used up all your mixture. The breadcrumbs get clumpy toward the end. Just do your best to coat the nuggets with crumbs of all sizes.

5. Bake the nuggets for 25 to 30 minutes, until they are lightly browned and crisp to your liking.

6. Serve warm dipped in ketchup or Green Goddess Sauce. And watch, everyone will be checkin' out what you are eating!

TIP:
Try modifying into a burger shape for a breaded checkin' patty!

CHICKPEA MASALA (CHOLE)

SERVES 4

1 medium onion, finely chopped (about 1 cup)

¼ teaspoon mustard seeds

Pinch of asafetida, optional

3 large tomatoes

½–1 small green finger pepper, seeded

1 tablespoon minced fresh ginger (see note)

2 cloves garlic

2 tablespoons chana masala powder

½ teaspoon cumin

½ teaspoon coriander

2 cups chickpeas, drained and rinsed (about 1½ cans)

2 cups cooked brown basmati rice

¼ cup cilantro, roughly chopped, for garnish

2 chives, chopped, for garnish

2 tablespoons finely chopped red onion, for garnish

Our friend Koyen once told us at the farmers market: "I love your plant-based recipes, but I miss Indian food." So true! While much of Indian cuisine is vegetarian, it is heavy on oil and ghee. We wanted to learn how to make Indian food that is plant-based. Luckily Koyen was up for the task: She fed us a number of recipes, took us on a field trip to an Indian grocery store, and sent rescue texts midrecipe. We are smitten with Indian cooking and the astounding amount of plants, flavors, and spices that are central to the cuisine! Chickpea Masala, a.k.a. Chole, was our first recipe with Koyen and is our current favorite. If you cannot find the ingredients for this recipe at your local market, it is absolutely worth a trip to an Indian grocery store. Use as much finger pepper as you like—we use less than half an inch and find that is enough heat for us.

1. In a large nonstick pan over medium-high heat, cook the onion until soft. Add tablespoons of water as needed if the pan gets too dry or the onions start to stick. Add the mustard seeds and a pinch of asafetida (if using) and continue stirring.

2. While the onions cook, in a food processor or high-speed blender, blend the tomatoes, finger pepper, ginger, and garlic until they've become a beautiful pink liquid.

3. Add the tomato mixture to the onions. Continue cooking for 8 minutes or so, until the sauce reduces and becomes thicker.

4. Add the chana masala powder, cumin, and coriander to the pan and stir as it cooks down. Cook for at least 8 minutes over medium heat and allow the sauce to slowly reduce and become thicker and darker.

5. Stir in the chickpeas. Reduce the heat to low and cook for 8 more minutes (be careful not to cook too long or the sauce will dry out).

6. Serve over a bed of brown rice and top with the cilantro, chives, and red onion.

NOTE:

Koyen stores ginger in her freezer pre-minced in ice cube trays!

BLACK RAMEN BOWL

Heart disease-friendly

MAKES 4 BOWLS

1 cup tiny potatoes
(the size of grapes)

2 heads baby bok choy, sliced

8 ounces mushrooms, sliced

1 medium red pepper, sliced

1 medium zucchini, quartered
lengthwise and sliced

½ cup shredded carrots

4 tablespoons miso
(we prefer white miso,
but any type will work)

4 tablespoons red curry paste
(we recommend Thai
Kitchen) or black bean
garlic sauce (we recommend
Lee Kum Kee)

4 tablespoons hoisin sauce
(we recommend Lee
Kum Kee)

8 ounces tofu, cubed

10 ounces black ramen
noodles (we prefer Lotus
Foods Forbidden Rice
Ramen)

4 green onions, sliced into
1-inch matchsticks,
for garnish

It is so soothing to watch Brian build these bowls. First, he adds the sauces to the base of each bowl, then the cooked veggies, cooked potatoes, and raw tofu cubes. The tofu looks so clean and expectant. It's like watching someone fold laundry—creating peaceful order out of chaos. Then, the dramatic black noodles and hot water transform it all into a savory, flavory Black Ramen Bowl.

1. Preheat the oven to 350°F. Line a small pan with parchment paper. Place the potatoes in a single layer on the pan and roast for 20 minutes, or until cooked through. Some potatoes may even pop, and those are my favorite crispy bites if I can eat them before Ann. Remove the potatoes from the oven, halve each one, and set aside.

2. In a large nonstick pan over medium-high heat, cook and stir the bok choy, mushrooms, red pepper, zucchini, and carrots until they begin to brown—2–3 minutes tops. Set aside.

3. In each bowl, place 1 tablespoon of miso, 1 tablespoon of red curry paste, and 1 tablespoon of hoisin sauce. We love the way the bowls look at this stage—so colorful and exciting.

4. To each of the bowls, add one-quarter of the vegetables, tofu cubes, and baby potato halves.

5. Bring a large pot of water to a boil and add the ramen. Use a chopstick or fork to gently poke and swirl the noodle bricks until they separate. Boil for 5 minutes or until the noodles are fully cooked.

6. Remove the pan from the heat, but do not drain! Using tongs or just two forks, serve a heap of ramen noodles directly from the pot into each of the four bowls. With a measuring cup or ladle, scoop about ½ cup of hot water from the pot into each bowl.

7. Stir each bowl thoroughly and deeply to make sure the sauces dissolve. Garnish with the green onions and serve hot.

SAN FRAN SAVORY BOWL

Heart disease-friendly

SERVES 5-6

2 Japanese sweet potatoes (about 4 cups) or Yukon Gold potatoes, cut in ½-inch cubes

4 large carrots, sliced in ½-inch rounds (about 3 cups)

16 ounces whole baby bella or white mushrooms, halved or quartered if very large

4 cups vegetable broth

½ cup nutritional yeast

4 tablespoons oat flour or any flour of choice

1 tablespoon curry powder

1 tablespoon garlic powder

1 teaspoon turmeric

1 tablespoon chopped fresh ginger

2 tablespoons white miso

Pinch of cayenne pepper

¼–½ teaspoon ground black pepper, to taste

1 large bunch of kale or other greens, stems stripped and leaves torn into large pieces

2 cups brown rice, cooked according to the package directions

1 large head broccoli, broken into spears, steamed until bright green

This glorious meal in one is both delicious and gorgeous! It was inspired by a bowl Ann and Essy had in the San Francisco airport of all places! Japanese sweet potatoes are white and one of our favorite sweet potatoes. Ann says this lovely bowl is full of everything healthy you could possibly find in your kitchen.

1. In a wok or large pan over medium-high heat, bring about 2 inches of water to a boil. Add the sweet potatoes, carrots, and mushrooms and cook, covered, at a brisk simmer, about 10 minutes, or until the sweet potatoes and carrots are just tender.

2. While the vegetables are cooking, place the vegetable broth, nutritional yeast, flour, curry powder, garlic powder, turmeric, ginger, miso, and cayenne pepper in a large pot or casserole dish and bring to a boil, stirring constantly. Immediately turn the heat to low and stir until the mixture thickens into a gravy.

3. Remove the sweet potatoes, carrots, and mushrooms with a slotted spoon and add to the gravy. Do not discard the cooking water—it is very flavorful and a good addition if the vegetable liquid is low.

4. Add the black pepper and kale to the gravy and vegetable mixture (if you are using spinach, add it just before serving; you can also add the kale just before serving if you want to keep it looking green), gently stir, and simmer about 4 minutes, or until the kale is just tender.

5. To serve, place a scoop of rice into individual bowls and top with the vegetables and gravy, with the bright green broccoli nestled on top.

6. The broth from the vegetables is delicious and adding a cup at the end makes the gravy more plentiful and even tastier.

BRIAN'S RED BEAN CHILI

Heart disease-friendly

SERVES 8-10

1 onion, chopped

1 zucchini, chopped

1 yellow squash, chopped

1 green bell pepper, chopped

8 ounces mushrooms, sliced

½ cup shredded carrots

1–2 cups shredded kale

15 ounces canned red beans, drained and rinsed

Two 15-ounce cans dark kidney beans, drained and rinsed

28 ounces canned whole peeled tomatoes, drained and cut into halves or thirds using scissors

28 ounces canned diced tomatoes

½ cup barbecue sauce, your favorite

2–3 tablespoons chili powder

1 tablespoon garlic powder

1 tablespoon onion powder

¼ teaspoon liquid smoke

1 tablespoon maple syrup

Brian's chili is dependably a standout hit. A constant. Even though his recipe constantly changes.

1. In a large soup pot over medium-high heat, add the onions and cook until translucent, about 2–3 minutes. Add 1 to 2 tablespoons of water if the pan gets too dry or the onions start to stick. Add the zucchini, yellow squash, green pepper, mushrooms, carrots, and kale and stir for a few minutes.

2. Reduce the heat to medium and add the red beans, kidney beans, whole tomatoes, diced tomatoes, barbecue sauce, chili powder, garlic powder, onion powder, liquid smoke, and maple syrup. Continue to cook, stirring occasionally. As you stir, taste the chili—add a bit more spice, liquid smoke, or barbecue sauce as needed. Reduce the heat to low and simmer for 10 minutes, or until ready to serve.

JIM'S KUNG PAO CHICKPEAS OVER BROWN RICE

Heart disease-friendly

SERVES 3–4

1 large onion, diced

1 red bell pepper, diced

Two 15-ounce cans no-salt chickpeas, aquafaba (bean water) reserved

1 tablespoon low-sodium tamari

2 tablespoons balsamic vinegar (see page 95)

4 cloves garlic, minced, or 1 teaspoon garlic powder

1 tablespoon chopped fresh ginger

1 teaspoon red pepper flakes, or to taste

4 green onions, chopped

½ cup parsley, chopped, for garnish

Cooked brown or black rice, for serving

Cooked kale or fresh greens, for serving (page 49)

Jim McNamara is a patient who has had a dramatic health turnaround on the *Prevent and Reverse Heart Disease* diet. He often shares his remarkable testimonial at Dr. Esselstyn's monthly seminars for heart disease patients at the Cleveland Clinic Center for Integrative and Lifestyle Medicine. This is his favorite dinner recipe and we understand why he loves it; it is *fast* to prepare and best of all, it is incredibly delicious! We make it on the stovetop in a casserole dish, while Jim makes it in a slow cooker for three hours on high heat or six hours on low heat. Try it any way you wish. The leftovers are great in a wrap.

1. In a medium pot, place the onion, red bell pepper, chickpeas, and reserved liquid. Add the tamari, vinegar, garlic, ginger, red pepper flakes, and green onions and stir well.

2. Cover and cook on low heat for 2 to 4 hours, or until you can't wait to eat any longer. The longer it cooks, the better it gets. Add the parsley and serve over brown or black rice with a big serving of cooked kale or fresh greens. If you are so lucky as to have leftovers, try stuffing some in a pita pocket or create a wrap, messy but good!

CHEEZY CHICKPEAS

Heart disease-friendly

SERVES 2–3

15 ounces canned no-salt or low-sodium chickpeas, aquafaba (bean water) reserved

1 teaspoon low-sodium tamari

½ cup nutritional yeast

1 tablespoon whole wheat flour or oat flour

1 teaspoon garlic powder

1 teaspoon onion powder

In her role as one of the coaches for the Rescue 10x Behavioral Change Program and curator of creative content at Plant-Strong, Ami Mackey helps others develop positive habits that last a lifetime. This recipe will undoubtedly become a favorite and change habits! It is sooo similar to mac and cheese, and it is one of Ami's most beloved recipes.

Try Cheezy Chickpeas alone, over brown rice, over whole-grain pasta, over greens, over a baked potato—over anything!

In a small pot, place the aquafaba and tamari, then whisk in the nutritional yeast, flour, garlic powder, and onion powder until well combined. Simmer over medium heat until the mixture thickens, stirring constantly. Remove from the heat, add the chickpeas, and stir to coat.

TIP:

Add your favorite fresh or frozen vegetables, such as peas, carrots, or corn.

VARIATIONS:

*For Nacho Cheezy Chickpeas: Add 1 teaspoon cumin and 1 teaspoon chili powder.

*For Buffalo Cheezy Chickpeas: Add 1 teaspoon hot sauce (we recommend Frank's Red Hot Sauce) and ½ teaspoon celery seed.

PLANT-BASED PAD THAI

To make heart disease-friendly: Leave out the avocado

SERVES 3–4

PAD THAI SAUCE

3 tablespoons low-sodium tamari

2 tablespoons rice vinegar

2 tablespoons maple syrup

1 tablespoon tamarind puree or ketchup (with no added high fructose corn syrup)

½ teaspoon hot sauce, optional

NOODLES

8 ounces pad thai–style brown rice noodles

1 cup onion, sliced into half-moons

3 cloves garlic, minced

8 ounces extra-firm tofu, cubed

¾ cup julienned carrots

½ red bell pepper, julienned

½ cup thinly sliced purple cabbage

3 green onions, chopped

1–2 cups mung bean sprouts, optional

½ cup cilantro, roughly chopped

The evening and dinner are etched in memory: I was in Boulder, Colorado, with my brother Zeb while our pal Morgan recounted a dramatic rock climbing accident and rescue, all while I tried pad thai for the first time. I feasted on every nail-biting detail of the story and every delicious bite of my pad thai. Re-creating a plant-based version for this book was top of the list, and it turns out it's easy to swap out eggs and meat for tofu. There are four important steps to this recipe and good timing helps. Try to coordinate cooking the noodles in the final minutes the vegetables and tofu are cooking.

1. Make the pad thai sauce (see tip): In a small bowl, whisk together the tamari, rice vinegar, maple syrup, tamarind puree, and hot sauce (if using). Set aside.

2. Make the noodles: Bring a large pot of water to a boil. Add the pad thai noodles and cook according to the package directions. (If possible, aim to do this when the vegetables and tofu are cooking in next step below.)

3. In a large nonstick pan over medium-high heat, cook the onion until translucent, about 3 minutes. If the pan gets dry, add a tablespoon of water. Add the garlic and continue stirring for another minute or two before adding the tofu, carrots, red pepper, purple cabbage, and green onions. If the pan gets too dry, add 1 tablespoon of water at a time as needed.

4. Drain the noodles. When the vegetables are tender but still a bit crisp and bright in color, add the noodles to the pan along with the pad thai sauce (if you doubled the sauce, save some for those who seek to add more, and for any leftovers). Mix and toss everything together.

recipe and ingredients continue

1 avocado, cubed, optional

½ cup coarsely chopped
dry-roasted peanuts
(no oil or salt added)

1 lime, cut into wedges

5. Plate each serving with a heap of mung bean sprouts (if using), a sprinkle of cilantro, avocado (if using), a handful of chopped peanuts, and a wedge of lime.

TIP:

Consider doubling the amount of sauce. We find we like the option of having a bit extra for drizzling on the dish during the meal, or for any leftovers, as the noodles tend to absorb the sauce in the fridge.

SWEET POTATO and CASHEW RICOTTA LASAGNA

To make heart disease-friendly: Substitute 2 cups firm tofu for the cashews

SERVES 12

2 cups raw cashews

1 onion, chopped

2 cloves garlic, minced

1 zucchini, cubed

1 cup shredded carrots

8 ounces mushrooms, sliced

1 red bell pepper, diced

10 ounces frozen spinach, thawed

1 tablespoon dried oregano

1 tablespoon dried thyme, or to taste

1 tablespoon dried basil

1 teaspoon onion powder

1 teaspoon garlic powder

2 teaspoons apple cider vinegar

6–8 cups (one recipe) Original Marinara (page 84) or three 25-ounce jars of marinara of choice (with no added oil)

Brian makes a mean lasagna, and best of all, he adds delicious new tweaks each time. However, we called "FREEZE" after this version. It needed to be shared! And made again! Combining the cooked veggies, spices, and cashew ricotta into the filling creates a texture and flavor we could not stop eating. Seriously, Ann and I each had three pieces!

1. Preheat the oven to 350°F.

2. In a medium bowl, soak the cashews—in enough hot water to cover them by about an inch—for at least 10 minutes.

3. In a large pan over medium-high heat, cook the onion until translucent, about 3 minutes. Turn the heat to medium and add the garlic, zucchini, carrots, mushrooms, red pepper, spinach, oregano, thyme, and basil and cook until the vegetables are tender and fragrant, about 5 minutes. Set aside.

4. Drain the cashews and place in a food processor or high-speed blender. Add the onion powder, garlic powder, and vinegar and blend to create the smooth cashew ricotta.

5. Transfer the cashew ricotta to the pan of vegetables. Stir until the cashew ricotta and vegetables are uniformly mixed.

6. In the bottom of a large lasagna pan (ours is 11½ × 17½ inches), spread a layer of marinara sauce, then add an even layer of uncooked noodles.

7. On top of the noodles, spread half of the cashew ricotta and vegetable mixture.

8. Top with another layer of sauce and another layer of noodles.

recipe and ingredients continue

2 boxes whole wheat lasagna noodles or rice lasagna noodles (we recommend Tinkyáda brand)

2 large sweet potatoes, cooked, peeled, and mashed (about 3 cups)

2 tomatoes, thinly sliced

9. On the second layer of noodles, spread the mashed sweet potato and top with a thin layer of sauce.

10. Then, add another layer of noodles and spread the remaining cashew ricotta and vegetable mixture on top.

11. Add another layer of sauce and place the final layer of noodles on top.

12. Spread the sauce over the noodles and add the tomato slices on top of the whole lasagna. If you wish, add a sprinkle of your favorite herbs as well—we use oregano and basil.

13. Cover with foil and cook for 60 minutes, removing the foil for the last 10 minutes. Cool for a few minutes before serving.

ANN'S OPEN-FACED TWICE-BAKED POTATOES

Heart disease-friendly

SERVES 4-6

1 large Japanese sweet potato

6 medium Yukon Gold potatoes

1 large sweet onion, cut into 8 chunks

6 large cloves garlic

6 tablespoons nutritional yeast

Pinch of cayenne pepper

½ teaspoon ground black pepper

1 cup unsweetened almond milk or other nondairy milk or vegetable broth, plus more as needed

1 bunch kale, stems removed, leaves chopped and cooked (4-6 cups before cooking) or greens of choice

3 green onions, chopped

Sweet or smoked paprika, for garnish

These are so good—you'll even eat the hide! Actually, Ann demands we all eat the hide as the skin is loaded with nutrients. These potatoes are central to one of our favorite meals for guests and grandchildren's birthday parties. Use whatever greens you prefer. Once, we had only two bunches of carrots with tops so we cut those tops up finely and they were perfect in the potatoes. Be inventive! Serve with one of Ann's Arugula Salads (pages 159–63) and asparagus.

1. Preheat the oven to 400°F. Line a sheet pan with parchment paper.

2. Poke a knife in each potato before baking. Place all the potatoes on the parchment-lined sheet pan.

3. Wrap the onion chunks and peeled whole garlic cloves together in foil. If you wish, place a layer of parchment paper between the foil and the onion and garlic. Place the onion and garlic bundle on the sheet pan along with the potatoes and bake for an hour, or until the potatoes are soft.

4. Carefully unwrap the onion and garlic bundle and place into a food processor. Be sure to include all the liquid. Blend until smooth (this will be most of the liquid for the potatoes).

5. Once the potatoes are cool enough to handle, cut them in half, scoop out the flesh, and place it in a large bowl. Place the empty Yukon Gold potato skins in a baking dish.

6. With a fork or potato masher, mash the Yukon Gold potatoes and sweet potato until smooth.

7. Stir in the onion and garlic liquid along with the nutritional yeast, cayenne, and pepper. Add the almond milk as needed. Stir in the kale and green onions.

8. Add more almond milk if the potatoes seem too thick. You may need a cup or more because nutritional yeast tends to absorb moisture.

9. Fill each Yukon Gold potato skin with the potato mixture, sprinkle with the paprika, and bake for 30 minutes, until piping hot.

PETER'S GLAZED EGGPLANT CUTLET with BROWN RICE

Heart disease–friendly

SERVES 2–3

3 tablespoons white miso

1 tablespoon mirin

1 tablespoon low-sodium tamari

1 large eggplant or 2 smaller eggplants

Sprinkle of sesame seeds, optional

2 cups cooked brown jasmine rice

2 green onions, chopped, for garnish

This miso-glazed eggplant dish came to us from a friend living in Australia. His teenagers love it, so we knew it had to be a crowd-pleaser. And it definitely is. A pile of brown rice and a heap of steamed broccoli round this dish out. You can also serve this meal with Green Beans with Sesame Crumble (page 179) and one of Ann's Arugula Salads (pages 159–63).

If there is any extra glaze, dab the broccoli in it. If you do not have an eggplant around, try this glaze on cauliflower slabs or cutlets.

1. Preheat the oven to 400°F. Line a sheet pan with parchment paper.

2. In a small bowl, mix the miso, mirin, tamari, and 1 tablespoon water until well combined with a glaze-like texture. Set aside.

3. Slice the eggplant lengthwise in cutlets ⅓ inch thick. Leave the skin around the edges of each slab. Try to remove the skin from the first and last slabs so the white shows (we think of this layer like heels of bread).

4. Using a knife, score the white surface in a grid pattern of small squares. We like to angle our grid on the diagonal.

5. In a large nonstick pan over medium heat, cook the eggplant cutlets for about 4 minutes, then flip and cook for another 4 minutes, or until the eggplant softens and browns a bit. The key is to make sure the eggplant is no longer spongy.

6. Transfer the eggplant cutlets to the prepared pan. Brush the miso glaze on top of each cutlet until all the surfaces are thinly coated.

7. Sprinkle the eggplant with the sesame seeds (if using). Place the pan in the oven for 2 to 4 minutes. Keep a close eye on it, removing it from the oven when the glaze starts to brown and bubble (this happens fast).

8. Serve with the brown rice and garnish with the green onions.

CREAMY STUFFED SWEET POTATOES

Heart disease–friendly

SERVES 2–4

1 very large sweet potato, preferably Garnet, an orange-fleshed sweet potato

1 very large Japanese sweet potato

4 tablespoons nutritional yeast

2 teaspoons minced fresh ginger or 1 teaspoon ground ginger

½ cup vegetable broth, plus more as needed

2 cups thawed frozen corn

2 green onions, chopped

¼ cup chopped red bell pepper

¼ cup cilantro, chopped, for garnish

The combination of orange sweet potatoes and Japanese sweet potatoes makes these Creamy Stuffed Sweet Potatoes so good. After baking, the skins of the potatoes are just as delicious as the filling. Japanese sweet potatoes have creamy-colored flesh with reddish-purple skin. These potatoes are particularly attractive baked and served individually in small oval baking dishes. Serve with asparagus or broccoli and a big salad or Rainbow Bean Slaw (page 151) and you'll have a beautiful dinner of gorgeous color.

1. Preheat the oven to 400°F. Line a sheet pan with parchment paper.

2. Poke a hole in each sweet potato, place on the prepared pan, and bake for 1 hour, or until soft when gently squeezed.

3. Once the sweet potatoes are cooked and cool enough to handle, place them on a cutting board and carefully cut each in half lengthwise.

4. With a spoon, gently scoop the flesh into a large bowl, leaving a little potato in the skin so the walls don't collapse.

5. With a potato masher or fork, mash the potatoes together until well combined and smooth.

6. Add the nutritional yeast, ginger, and vegetable broth and keep mashing until the potatoes are well mixed. Depending on your potatoes, you may need more or less broth.

7. Stir in the corn, green onions, and red pepper and carefully fill each of the potato skins.

8. Bake for 30 minutes, or until warmed and just beginning to bubble and brown. Garnish with the cilantro.

GINGERED CHICKPEAS and ROASTED CHERRY TOMATOES OVER BLACK RICE

Heart disease–friendly

SERVES 4-6

2 pints cherry tomatoes
(about 4 cups)

2 tablespoons balsamic vinegar
(see page 95)

½ teaspoon ground black pepper

1 large sweet onion, halved and
thinly sliced

1 heaping tablespoon minced
fresh ginger

1 teaspoon turmeric

1 teaspoon cumin

Two 15-ounce cans no-salt
chickpeas, aquafaba
(bean water) reserved

1 cup vegetable broth or water

⅓ cup nutritional yeast

2 tablespoons lime juice

Zest of ½ lime

1 bunch cilantro, roughly chopped
(nearly 2 cups), or parsley

1½ cups black rice, cooked

This is such a colorful dish and so quick and easy to make. Serve over black rice or any whole grain or with broccoli and a salad. If you can't find chickpeas with no salt added, rinse and drain them, and then add an extra cup of vegetable broth instead of the aquafaba, which will have high salt content.

1. Preheat the oven to 400°F. Line a sheet pan with parchment paper.

2. Place the cherry tomatoes on the prepared pan and sprinkle with the balsamic vinegar and black pepper. Transfer the pan to the middle rack in the oven and roast for 15 minutes, or until the tomatoes begin to brown a little and collapse.

3. Meanwhile, in a large pan over medium-high heat, cook the onions, stirring frequently, until they begin to brown. If the pan gets dry, add a tablespoon of water as needed. Add the ginger, turmeric, and cumin and reduce the heat to medium. Stir a few minutes to combine the flavors.

4. Add the chickpeas, reserved aquafaba, and vegetable broth and bring the mixture just to a boil. Reduce the heat to low, cover, and simmer for about 10 minutes.

5. Stir in the roasted tomatoes, nutritional yeast, lime juice, and lime zest, and cook another few minutes.

6. Add the cilantro, admire the beautiful colors. Serve over a heap of black rice and enjoy this gorgeous, tasty dish!

SHEPHERDESS PIE
toptopped with **TATTIES** and **NEEPS**

Heart disease-friendly

SERVES 4

TATTIES AND NEEPS

4 cups cubed Yukon Gold potatoes

2 cups cubed turnips (and/or rutabaga)

½ cup unsweetened almond milk, plus more as needed

¼ cup nutritional yeast, or to taste

1 teaspoon garlic powder

½ teaspoon salt, optional, or 1 tablespoon low-sodium tamari

Cracked black pepper, to taste

Tatties and neeps may sound like the beginning of some middle-school boy joke, but they are actually a Scottish reference to potatoes and turnips. We love tatties and neeps on this side of the pond, too!

Now, which sounds more alluring? A tatties and neeps–topped lentil-pie dinner with a shepherd—or with a shepherdess? Hmm, just as we suspected. Serve with one of Ann's Arugula Salads (pages 159–63). Slainte!

1. Make the tatties and neeps: Place the potatoes and turnips in a large pot. Cover with water and boil until tender, about 10 minutes. Drain and place in a large bowl. Mash with a potato masher or a fork.

FILLING

1 cup diced onion

1 clove garlic, minced

8 ounces mushrooms, sliced, optional

1 cup sliced carrots (about 2 carrots)

½ cup frozen or fresh peas

½ cup cooked brown lentils, or more if you don't use mushrooms

1 bay leaf

1 cup low-sodium vegetable broth

2 teaspoons white miso or any lighter miso

2 teaspoons tomato paste

2 tablespoons whole wheat or oat flour

1 tablespoon low-sodium tamari

2 teaspoons dried thyme

1 teaspoon dried crushed rosemary

2. Add the almond milk, nutritional yeast, garlic powder, salt (if using), and black pepper and mash until smooth. You may need to add a bit more liquid than you expect since the nutritional yeast soaks up some of it. Taste to see if you need more nutritional yeast, salt, or pepper. Set aside.

3. Make the filling: In a large pan over medium-high heat, add the onion, stirring frequently until it becomes translucent and browns a bit—about 3 minutes. Add a splash of water to the pan if the bottom gets dry. Add the garlic and mushrooms (if using) and continue cooking and stirring until the mushrooms soften and cook down, then add the carrots, peas, lentils, bay leaf, and broth. To a small bowl add the miso, tomato paste, flour, and tamari, and stir until dissolved, then pour into the pan and continue simmering to a thickness of your liking. Add the thyme and rosemary and stir.

4. Preheat the oven to 350°F. In a baking dish (9 × 13 inches or equivalent), layer the filling on the bottom and place the tatties and neeps on top. Bake for 30 minutes.

CHAPTER 12

DREAMY, DARING, and DELICIOUS

We knew we had a book squarely for Plant-Based Women Warriors when early in the project we tallied the number of recipes in each section: roughly eight in the breakfast section and about the same in the lunch and soup sections. Then we counted the dessert section—we had forty-four recipes! Boom! On the right track creating our cookbook for plant-based, dessert-loving Women Warriors (and about thirty-four made it into the book)!

PEPPARKAKOR (CRISPY SWEDISH GINGER COOKIE)

Heart disease-friendly

**MAKES ABOUT
18–24 COOKIES,
DEPENDING ON SIZE**

1 cup oat flour or whole wheat pastry flour

¼ teaspoon baking soda

¼ teaspoon baking powder

¼ teaspoon ground black pepper

¼ teaspoon cinnamon

Pinch of ground cloves

½ cup maple syrup

2 tablespoons molasses

1 tablespoon fresh ginger (use a Microplane or finely, finely mince it) or ½ teaspoon ground ginger

1 tablespoon apple cider vinegar

Swedish custom says you place a pepparkakor in your palm, make a wish, then tap the cookie with one finger. If the cookie breaks into three pieces, your wish will come true. If it doesn't break into three the first time, do what we do: Eat the broken one and keep trying with more and more cookies. Pepper—yes, black pepper—is a distinguishing feature of this unique Swedish treat.

1. Preheat the oven to 350°F. Line a sheet pan with parchment paper.

2. In a small bowl, combine the oat flour, baking soda, baking powder, black pepper, cinnamon, and cloves. Add the maple syrup, molasses, ginger, and vinegar and stir until smooth. Note: This batter is more liquidy than most cookie batters. Spoon the batter onto the prepared pan into silver dollar–size dollops. Be careful not to make them too big—otherwise, they won't get crispy.

3. Bake for 16 to 18 minutes, or until uniformly crisp. (If you have an oven that runs hot, keep a close eye on these—some people report they are done after 10 minutes.) Allow the cookies to cool for 5 to 10 minutes; that's how they get their snappy crispiness. Think of your wish!

PEPPARKAKOR

AMARETTO COOKIES

CRISPY VANILLA WAFERS

CUT-OUT
OATMEAL
COOKIES

AMARETTO COOKIES

3 tablespoons flaxseed meal

1 cup maple syrup

1–3 tablespoons almond extract, to taste (some prefer more of an amaretto flavor and some less)

2 teaspoons orange zest (from about 1 orange)

¾ cup oat flour

1½ cups almond flour (also called almond meal)

½ teaspoon baking powder

Pinch of salt, optional

24 raw whole almonds, more or less as needed (1 per cookie)

TIP:

For crispier cookies, turn the oven off, but open the door and leave the cookies in for one more minute. Check for crispiness and return to the oven for a minute more, if needed.

These cookies may have a Proustian effect on you! The secret is the amaretto flavor from the almond extract in these treats. It is stunning how many say, "Oh wait, let me smell that again; it reminds me of something," the way the narrator in Proust's novel *Remembrance of Things Past* bites into a petite madeleine cookie and it triggers a flood of deep childhood memories.

Ann likes these crispy, so we always push them to the edge and almost burn them. So scary. (See the tip.) If you prefer a softer cookie, just decrease the cook time. We knew we had a winner when our granddaughter/niece ate fifteen of these in one evening! Nothing like a twelve-year-old's approval.

1. Preheat the oven to 375°F. Line a sheet pan with parchment paper.

2. In a small bowl, combine the flaxseed meal and ¼ cup water. Let the mixture sit for 3 to 5 minutes while it thickens.

3. In large bowl, combine the maple syrup, flaxseed mixture, almond extract, and orange zest until well combined. Add the oat flour, almond flour, baking powder, and salt (if using) and mix.

4. Using a spoon to create cookies roughly 2 inches in diameter, scoop the batter onto the prepared pan. Place an almond into the center of each cookie. Bake for 12 to 14 minutes, until lightly browned and crisp—be careful not to burn.

CRISPY VANILLA WAFERS

Heart disease-friendly

MAKES 36

½ cup oat flour

¼ teaspoon baking powder

⅓ cup maple syrup

½ teaspoon vanilla

1 teaspoon apple cider vinegar

1 teaspoon lemon juice

These cookies were inspired by the delicious little droplets of batter that fall between the wells of cupcake pans. When baked, they are like teeny, tiny crisp cookies. They also remind us of the Nilla Wafers we used to love. Pair them with Gingered Minty Melon Balls in Orange Juice (page 285) or any of our Puddings (pages 303 and 307) or Gelatos (page 305).

1. Preheat the oven to 350°F. Line a sheet pan with parchment paper. Be sure the paper is lying absolutely flat or the cookies will spread into one another. It helps to scrunch up the parchment paper first, then flatten it in the pan.

2. In a large bowl, combine the oat flour and baking powder.

3. Add the maple syrup, vanilla, vinegar, lemon juice, and 1 tablespoon water and stir until smooth (the batter will be very liquidy compared to most cookie batters).

4. Spoon silver dollar–size dollops of the batter (approximately 1 teaspoon) onto the prepared pan. Be careful not to make them too big—otherwise, they won't get crispy.

5. Bake for about 14 minutes, or until browned around the edges. Keep a close eye on them—in some ovens, they can take as little as 8 minutes to bake.

6. Allow the cookies to cool and get crispy on the cookie sheet, then carefully remove them from the parchment paper with a spatula. If you have any leftovers, seal tightly and store in a cool, dry place.

VARIATION: CAT IN THE HAT DESSERT STACK

Stack Raspberry Pudding (page 307) in between layers of Crispy Vanilla Wafers (so they resemble the striped hat worn by the Dr. Seuss character the Cat in the Hat). Or try layering with Lemon, Lime, Strawberry, Chocolate, and Mint Chocolate Pudding (pages 307 and 303).

CUT-OUT OATMEAL COOKIES
and
GRANOLA BITS

MAKES ONE SHEET PAN OF SHAPES AND BITS OF GRANOLA, SIZES OF YOUR CHOICE

1⅓ cups walnuts

⅔ cup maple syrup

½ teaspoon vanilla

¼ teaspoon cinnamon

¼ teaspoon ground cardamom, optional

¼ teaspoon nutmeg

2½ cups old-fashioned rolled oats

⅓ cup raisins

Optional add-ins: dried cranberries, dried cherries, pistachios, pecans, walnuts, or nondairy chocolate chips

Imagine if granola, oatmeal raisin cookies, and sugar cookies mated in a plant-based universe. These are crispy cut-out cookies that satisfy! And all the bits and pieces around the cookie shapes remain on the pan and bake into the granola bits. This supports my favorite theory that granola really is cookie crumbles.

1. Preheat the oven to 350°F. Line a sheet pan with parchment paper.

2. In a food processor or high-speed blender, blend the walnuts with ¼ cup water until clumps form. Add the maple syrup, vanilla, cinnamon, cardamom (if using), and nutmeg and blend until well combined. The batter should be thick yet pourable.

3. In a large bowl, place the oats, raisins, and any add-in options of your choice. Add the batter and mix until everything is evenly coated.

4. Place the mixture onto the prepared pan and flatten so that it is about ¼ to ⅓ inch thick. Try to make it as even as possible to ensure the cookies bake evenly. With a cookie cutter or a drinking glass, cut out cookie shapes and leave the scraps (bits and pieces around the cookie shapes) on the pan, too. These in-between pieces are the granola bits.

5. Bake for 24 to 26 minutes, until slightly browned and crispy. On humid days we have to leave them in a few minutes longer, sometimes with the oven off, for around 5 minutes to crisp up.

LIME LOVES WATERMELON

and

WATERMELON LOVES LIME

Heart disease-friendly

MAKES AS MANY CUBES AS YOU WISH TO CHOP, AND VARIES PER WATERMELON SIZE

1 watermelon, rind removed, sliced into sections, chopped into cubes, or scooped into balls

Zest of 1–2 limes

1–2 limes, juiced

Pinch of chili powder, optional

The best way to choose a watermelon is by its weight: Heaviest is best. The next things to look for are:

*A yellowish area on the exterior, which shows it was grown on the ground and in the sun.

*Sugar lines, which are light, scratchy lines on the exterior that look like light brown stitches, where the sweetness is getting out.

*A dimple or a puckered scarred area that has healed over. This means the watermelon is a sweet one and bees were trying to get in at some point. This one is a find!

And the best way to eat watermelon is with a kiss of lime! You will delight in the bright flavor.

If you are feeling game, add a wee pinch of chili powder, which adds a whole new twist, making it more of an appetizer than a dessert!

In a large bowl, place the watermelon and then top with the zest and juice of 1 lime. As you eat the cubes, continue drizzling lime juice and adding lime zest from a second lime if needed—you want to be sure to cover each piece! If interested, add a pinch of chili powder for a savory pungent twist.

PEACH MELBA

Heart disease–friendly

SERVES 8

4 fresh peaches, or canned if fresh peaches are not available

One 10-ounce package frozen raspberries, slightly thawed

1 tablespoon raspberry balsamic vinegar, optional (see page 95)

12 ounces lite firm silken tofu (see note)

⅓ cup maple syrup

3 tablespoons lime juice

Zest of 1 lime

Traditionally, peach melba is made with fresh peaches and served with raspberry sauce and vanilla ice cream. This version has the peaches and the raspberry sauce, but instead of the vanilla ice cream, it is served with lime mousse! You will have extra raspberry sauce, which is good on waffles or pancakes, or drizzle it over any fruit or even over rice! In a pinch, canned peaches will work if peaches are not in season. This is oh so beautiful and delicious! It's so sad when summer ends and fresh peaches are gone.

1. Slice each peach into roughly 8 sections (peeling is optional).

2. In a food processor, place the raspberries and blend until smooth. Add the raspberry balsamic vinegar (if using) and blend again. Transfer the raspberry mixture to a bowl and set aside. Clean the food processor as we will use it again to make the mousse.

3. In the food processor, blend the tofu, maple syrup, lime juice, and lime zest until very smooth. Keep scraping down the sides of the processor to blend completely into a mousse. If you have time before assembling, refrigerate the mousse for at least 10 minutes.

4. To assemble, place about half of a sliced peach, roughly 4 sections, in each bowl. Cover with 2 to 3 tablespoons of lime mousse and then top with a tablespoon of raspberry sauce. There may be extra sauce—it is delicious with anything in the dessert section, especially cakes, cookies, or mousses!

NOTE:

It is important to use lite firm silken tofu in this recipe, as the firm silken texture is essential for the smoothness of the lime mousse. We recommend Mori-Nu Lite Firm.

GINGERED MINTY MELON BALLS in ORANGE JUICE

Heart disease–friendly

SERVES 4

1 cantaloupe, halved and seeded

½ cup fresh orange juice

1 teaspoon finely chopped fresh ginger

2 teaspoons chopped fresh mint, plus whole leaves for garnish

1 tablespoon dark chocolate balsamic vinegar (see page 95)

These are fresh tasting and delicious in summer or winter. Using a melon baller makes all the difference. The little round balls are exactly bite size and visually beautiful. Serve with Crispy Vanilla Wafers (page 278) for a knockout dessert.

With a melon baller, make melon balls and place them in a glass bowl if possible. Pour the orange juice over the melon almost to cover. Sprinkle with fresh ginger and mint. Garnish with whole mint leaves and drizzle with chocolate balsamic vinegar individually.

ZANDER TART

SERVES 4-6

12 ounces silken firm tofu (see notes)

1 cup pecans, lightly toasted, plus a few extra for garnish

⅔–¾ cup raisins

½ cup almond butter or walnut butter (see notes)

⅔ cup maple syrup, plus more as needed

½–⅔ cup thawed frozen raspberries

¼ cup lemon juice, plus more as needed

Zest of 1 lemon

Fresh berries of choice, for garnish

Zander Tart sounds like Linzer tart, the centuries-old bakery favorite. Yet, berries and nuts are where the similarities end. Our cheesecake-style tart received a big thumbs-up from its first taste-tester, our twenty-two-year-old pal Zander, and thus is duly named after him. Blending the raspberries into the filling makes it a delicious, pink wonder.

1. At least 8 hours ahead of time, tightly wrap the block of tofu in 6 to 8 dish towels and place in the fridge. Or, press your tofu in a tofu press to remove extra moisture. Ideally the tofu block will become roughly the texture of a block of cream cheese. This is an essential step to achieving a thick, creamy-textured tart.

2. Make the crust: In a high-speed blender, blend the pecans, raisins, and 2 tablespoons water. Blend until the mixture reaches a paste-like consistency or begins to slightly clump together. Scrape down the sides if needed. Remove and press evenly into a 7-inch springform pan, or a similar-size pan.

3. Clean the blender as you will use it again for the filling.

4. Make the filling: In the blender, blend the tofu, almond butter, maple syrup, frozen raspberries, and lemon juice until smooth. Taste and add more lemon juice or maple syrup, if needed.

5. Evenly spread the filling on top of the crust and chill for at least an hour before serving.

6. Just before serving, top with the lemon zest, fresh berries, and crumbled toasted pecans.

NOTES:

*It is important to use silken firm tofu in this recipe (not "lite"). We recommend Mori-Nu brand.

*Walnut butter can be hard to find. To make your own, blend walnuts in a high-speed blender until they become butter-like in texture.

LEMON PIE SQUARES

**MAKES ONE
9-INCH SQUARE PAN
OR ONE 9-INCH
PIE PLATE**

1½ cups pecans

1 cup golden raisins

1 cup old-fashioned rolled oats

2 tablespoons lemon zest (from about 2 lemons), a pinch reserved for garnish

½ cup lemon juice

6 tablespoons maple syrup

¼ teaspoon saffron, optional

½ recipe Lemon Frosting or Pudding (page 307), chilled

We dream of lemon squares. Cool and bright. We were thrilled to reinvent them this summer, in pie form, with an unlikely strategic ingredient—oatmeal! The saffron makes the squares a more vibrant shade of yellow.

1. Make the crust: Preheat the oven to 350°F. In a food processor or high-speed blender, blend the pecans, raisins, and 1 to 2 tablespoons water until the mixture reaches a paste-like consistency or begins to slightly clump together. Scrape down the sides if needed. Remove the mixture from the food processor and press evenly into the base of a 9 × 9-inch square pan or 9-inch pie plate. Bake for 10 to 12 minutes, until a bit toasty and fragrant. Set aside and let cool.

2. Make the filling: In a small pot over high heat, stir together the oats, 1⅔ cups water, lemon zest, lemon juice, maple syrup, and saffron (if using). Bring to a boil, then reduce the heat to low and simmer, uncovered, for about 5 minutes, or until the mixture looks like runny oatmeal. Blend in the pot with an immersion blender until completely smooth, or transfer to a blender or food processor and blend.

3. Pour the warm filling over the crust. Cover and chill for at least an hour or until it sets firm and does not squish when light pressure is applied. Remove from the fridge and spread a thick layer of Lemon Frosting or Pudding on top. Garnish with the reserved lemon zest. Cover and return to the fridge until ready to serve.

AMARETTO CHERRY CHOCOLATE HAZELNUT SCONES

MAKES 8

⅓ cup hazelnuts

1½ cups oat flour

1½ cups almond flour (also called almond meal)

1 tablespoon flaxseed meal

½ cup maple syrup

1 teaspoon vanilla extract

1–2 tablespoons almond extract, to taste (some prefer more of an amaretto flavor and some less)

⅓ cup nondairy chocolate chips

⅓ cup dried cherries

These are pure weaponry against hunger. Plus, they are addictive and decadent! Use them to slay the apprehensions of your plant-based-resistant pal, your hesitant neighbors, or your growing kids.

1. Preheat the toaster oven or oven to 325°F. Place the hazelnuts on a tray. Toast for 5 minutes, or until fragrant. Set aside.

2. Preheat the oven to 400°F. Line a sheet pan with parchment paper.

3. In a large bowl, combine the oat flour, almond flour, and flaxseed meal. Add the maple syrup, vanilla, almond extract, and 1 to 2 tablespoons water and gently fold the ingredients together until the dough forms into a solid clump. Fold in the chocolate chips, toasted hazelnuts, and dried cherries.

4. Press out the dough in the prepared pan into a 1-inch-thick circle (wetting your fingers a bit helps keep the dough from sticking). Use a pizza cutter or a sharp knife to cut the dough into wedges. Or, if you prefer round scones, use a spoon to scoop out dough for 10 scones.

5. Bake for 13 to 15 minutes, until browned on top. Keep an eye on them as they brown up quickly. Serve warm if possible.

CARDAMOM LEMON COURGETTE CAKE

Heart disease-friendly

MAKES ONE 9-INCH CAKE

¾ cup shredded zucchini, plus more for garnish

1½ cups whole wheat flour or oat flour

½ teaspoon baking powder

1 teaspoon baking soda

½ teaspoon ground cardamom, plus more for garnish

½ teaspoon cinnamon, plus more for garnish

1 tablespoon flaxseed meal

⅔ cup maple syrup

Zest of 1 lemon

Juice of 1 lemon (2–3 tablespoons juice)

½ teaspoon vanilla

½ recipe Lemon Frosting or Pudding (page 307); use whole recipe for a double-layer cake

A pal of mine says our Cardamom Lemon Courgette Cake sounds more like a stripper than a dessert! Take a risk and serve it topless—without any icing! This cake's exotic flavor comes from the lemon-cardamom blend and the courgette, a.k.a. zucchini, which gives it texture and keeps it moist! You can use whole wheat or oat flour, or a mix of your favorite flours. Our favorite way to celebrate with this cake is to frost it with Lemon Frosting or Pudding (page 307), or you can just enjoy it plain—topless—if that's your thing!

1. Preheat the oven to 350°F. Line a 9-inch cake pan with parchment paper (or use a nonstick or silicone pan).

2. If the zucchini releases lots of water when you shred it, lightly squeeze it in a dish towel.

3. In a large bowl, combine the flour, baking powder, baking soda, cardamom, cinnamon, and flaxseed meal. Add the shredded zucchini, maple syrup, ¼ cup water, lemon zest, lemon juice, and vanilla and mix until well combined.

4. Pour the batter into the prepared pan and bake for 35 minutes or until golden brown on top.

5. Frost with the Lemon Frosting or Pudding. Garnish with a dusting of cardamom and cinnamon and sprinkle with a few zucchini shreds.

ORANGE-LEMON CUPCAKES with LIME FROSTING

Heart disease-friendly

MAKES 12 CUPCAKES

1¾ cups oat flour

½ teaspoon baking soda

¼ teaspoon baking powder

½ cup maple syrup

Zest of 1 orange, a pinch reserved for garnish

Zest of 1 lemon, a pinch reserved for garnish

⅔ cup orange juice

⅓ cup lemon juice

½ recipe Lime Frosting or Pudding (page 307), or more if preferred

Zest of ¼ lime, for garnish

I wish I had recorded the shriek of delight when I brought these cupcakes over to my parents' house for them to taste. They hit *all* my mom's favorite buttons: lemon, lime, orange, acid, and cupcakes! I felt like such a proud child/baker!

1. Preheat the oven to 350°F. Locate a nonstick muffin or cupcake pan. (Liners will not work as the batter does not free itself from the paper.)

2. In a large bowl, combine the oat flour, baking soda, and baking powder.

3. In a small bowl, mix together the maple syrup, orange zest, lemon zest, orange juice, and lemon juice. Add the wet ingredients to the bowl with the dry ingredients and stir until mixed.

4. Pour the batter into the cupcake wells. Bake for 18 minutes or until lightly browned on top.

5. Once the cupcakes have cooled in the pan, remove from the wells and frost with Lime Frosting or Pudding. Right before serving, add the colorful trio of orange, lemon, and lime zest to the cupcakes.

OUTTA SIGHT BROWNIES

3 tablespoons flaxseed meal

1 cup walnuts

1¼ cups maple syrup

2 teaspoons vanilla

4 ounces unsweetened baking chocolate

2 tablespoons cocoa powder

1 cup oat flour

½ teaspoon baking soda

Pinch of salt, optional

VARIATION: MINT CHIP BROWNIES

Stir in ¼ teaspoon mint extract and ⅓ cup nondairy dark chocolate chips to the batter before baking.

VARIATION: CHERRY CHUNK WALNUT BROWNIES

Stir in ⅓ cup walnut pieces and ⅓ cup dried cherries to the batter before baking.

My favorite part of brownies is the batter. Gooey, rich, and chocolatey. Honestly, I prefer the batter raw, by the spoonful! If I had it my way, I wouldn't even bake brownies; I would just serve bowls of batter! And since I have such batter love, our recipe allows for many generous tastes of the (raw!) batter. (For those who do not make a meal out of tasting the raw batter, you can bake the extra in a ramekin.) Seriously, there will be extra batter. You're welcome.

1. Preheat the oven to 350°F. Line a 9 × 9-inch brownie pan with parchment paper (or use a nonstick pan) and also line one oven-safe ramekin (if you don't plan on eating the extra batter raw!) with parchment paper.

2. In a small bowl, mix the flaxseed meal with ¼ cup water. Let sit until it is egg-like in texture, about 5 minutes.

3. In a food processor, blend the walnuts with 3 tablespoons water. Scrape the sides of the processor down as needed and continue blending until the walnuts turn whitish and form a hummus-like textured clump. Add the flaxseed meal mixture, maple syrup, and vanilla, and blend until smooth.

4. In a double boiler, or in a microwave, melt the baking chocolate. Add the melted chocolate and cocoa powder to the mixture in the food processor and blend until smooth and well combined.

5. In a large bowl, combine the oat flour, baking soda, and salt (if using).

6. Add the flour mixture to the mixture in the food processor and blend until the mixture looks like brownie batter.

7. Pour the batter into the prepared pan (and the prepared ramekin, if you have extra raw batter) and bake for 35 to 40 minutes, or to your level of preferred gooeyness.

FROSTED FUDGY WALNUT BROWNIES

**MAKES ONE
9-INCH SQUARE PAN**

1½ cups walnut pieces

1½ cups maple syrup

⅔ cup cocoa powder

2 teaspoons vanilla

1 cup cooked, peeled sweet potato (about 1 sweet potato; see page 48)

¾ cup oat flour

1 teaspoon baking powder

Pinch of salt, optional

¼ cup add-ins, optional, your choice: walnut pieces, pecan pieces, nondairy chocolate chips, raisins, dried cherries, dried cranberries, or candied ginger

No one believes the spectacular frozen frosted fudge squares in *The Engine 2 Cookbook* are vegan or that they are made with sweet potatoes. We decided to carry that winning secret ingredient over to this brownie recipe, and the fun frosted feature, too!

1. Preheat the oven to 350°F. Prepare a 9 × 9-inch square pan with parchment paper or use a nonstick loaf pan.

2. In a food processor, blend the walnuts with ⅓ cup water until the mixture forms a clump. Add the maple syrup, cocoa powder, vanilla, and sweet potato and blend until smooth, about 1 minute.

3. Remove ⅓ cup of the mixture from the food processor and set aside. This will be your frosting.

4. To the remaining mixture in the food processor, add the oat flour, baking powder, and salt (if using) and blend until the mixture looks like brownie batter. If it seems too thick, add 1 to 2 tablespoons water and blend again. Go ahead and taste it at this stage (my favorite part). If you are using any add-ins, transfer the batter to a bowl and hand-stir them in.

5. Scoop the batter into the prepared pan. Bake for 30 minutes, or to your level of preferred gooeyness (baking time will be longer if using a loaf pan). Allow to cool for a few minutes before frosting. Slice and serve warm, if possible.

OUR CHOCOLATE CAKE

Heart disease-friendly

MAKES ONE 9-INCH CAKE

1½ cups oat flour

¼ cup cocoa powder

1 teaspoon baking soda

⅛ teaspoon cinnamon

⅔ cup maple syrup

6 tablespoons unsweetened applesauce

1 tablespoon apple cider vinegar

1 teaspoon vanilla

½ recipe frosting (see variations on page 302); use whole recipe for a double-layer cake

Our Chocolate Cake can be frosted in endless ways! There are as many variations as there are those hungry for cake. Below we offer a handful of suggestions for frosting layers. No matter which frosting you choose, you have full permission to create your own wonder: We suggest decorating the frosted layer with as much fresh fruit as you can muster—it makes a delicious, alluring addition. Tip: If you want a layer cake, double the recipe.

1. Preheat the oven to 350°F. Line a 9 × 9-inch square cake pan or 9-inch round cake pan with parchment paper.

2. In a large bowl, combine the flour, cocoa powder, baking soda, and cinnamon, and stir. Add the maple syrup, applesauce, vinegar, vanilla, and ¾ cup water. Using a hand mixer, mix until well combined (you can also use a stand mixer). Pour the batter into the prepared pan and bake for 30 minutes, until the cake surface is firm, not giving, to the touch in the center. Cool before frosting.

recipe continues

VARIATIONS:

To make heart disease–friendly: Use any of the frostings except the Peanut Butter and German Chocolate versions

This cake is delicious with any of the frostings below!

Creamy Chocolate Frosting
(page 303)

Our German Chocolate Frosting
(page 308)

Raspberry Frosting
(see Berry Frosting, page 307)

Blueberry Frosting
(see Berry Frosting, page 307)

Blackberry Frosting
(see Berry Frosting, page 307)

Peanut Butter Ganache
(page 305)

Mint Chocolate Chip Frosting
(page 303)

Strawberry Frosting
(see Berry Frosting, page 307)

CREAMY CHOCOLATE FROSTING *or* PUDDING

MAKES ABOUT 2 CUPS

Two 12-ounce packages silken firm or extra-firm tofu (see note)

6 tablespoons cocoa powder

⅔–¾ cup maple syrup, to taste

½ teaspoon vanilla

"This tastes like the Snack Pack pudding from my childhood!" is the best compliment we have received about this pudding. And we agree. To be honest, we make this recipe just a little differently each time: We might add more cocoa or a bit more maple syrup. Tweak the ingredients until this pudding sings to you and fills you with your own nostalgic memories! Ideally prepare the tofu a day in advance.

1. Drain the tofu and wrap both blocks in 6 to 8 absorbent dish towels or cloth napkins (it will feel like a well-bundled baby!). Place in the fridge and apply a bit of pressure to the blocks with a plate or other weight—it is okay if the tofu breaks into sections. Refrigerate for at least 24 hours to create a thicker consistency. You will notice the cloth napkins become soaked with water from the tofu; replace with fresh outer dish towels as needed.

2. In a food processor, place the tofu, cocoa, maple syrup, and vanilla. Blend until smooth and there are no visible small flecks of tofu. It will be a thick, creamy consistency ready to spread as frosting or eat as a pudding.

NOTE:

The tofu *must* be silken *and* firm or extra firm to work in this recipe. It's fine if it is also "lite."

VARIATION:
MINT CHOCOLATE CHIP FROSTING OR PUDDING

Add 1 to 2 teaspoons mint extract (depending on how strong a mint taste you like) and a sprinkle of nondairy chocolate chips.

PEANUT BUTTER GELATO or GANACHE

MAKES ABOUT 2½ CUPS

12 ounces silken extra-firm tofu (see note)

⅔ cup peanut butter

½ cup maple syrup

½ teaspoon vanilla

Pinch of salt, optional

Proceed with caution. This is smooth, creamy, sweet, and dreamy comfort food. Freeze it to make a gelato you'll weep over. Or if you are like Ann, don't bother to freeze it—spoon it right out of the food processor as a creamy ganache-textured treat!

Drain the tofu and wrap it in a dish towel. Squeeze until the dish towel gets wet. In a food processor or high-speed blender, place the tofu, peanut butter, maple syrup, vanilla, and salt (if using). Blend until creamy and smooth. Serve right away to enjoy as a ganache. To make gelato, seal in a lidded container and freeze until solid. Allow to thaw a bit before serving for that perfect gelato texture.

NOTE:

The tofu *must* be silken *and* extra firm to work in this recipe.

VARIATION: CHOCOLATE GELATO OR GANACHE

Use almond butter instead of peanut butter for less nut butter taste (though stick with peanut butter if you want that Reese's Peanut Butter Cup flavor) and add ½ cup cocoa powder.

VARIATION:

Try the mind-blowing combination of Peanut Butter Gelato and Chocolate Gelato gently swirled together!

BLUEBERRY
PUDDING

MINT
CHOCOLATE
CHIP
PUDDING,
page 303

BLACKBERRY
PUDDING

CREAMY
CHOCOLATE
PUDDING,
page 303

RASPBERRY
PUDDING

LIME
PUDDING

STRAWBERRY
PUDDING

LEMON
PUDDING

LIME FROSTING or PUDDING

MAKES ABOUT 2 CUPS

Two 12-ounce packages silken firm or extra-firm tofu (see note)

⅔–¾ cup maple syrup, to taste

Zest of 1 lime

2 limes, juiced (about 6 tablespoons)

This dessert is a blue ribbon bearer and has been our mainstay for decades. Ann presented us lime mousse with fresh fruit back in the '90s. Then, we soon caught on to the fact that firm silken tofu is also versatile as a frosting or a pudding, and most recently, we used it to make gelato (Peanut Butter Gelato, page 305). Our other frostings and puddings are descendants of this beauty! Ideally prepare the tofu a day in advance.

1. Drain the tofu and wrap both blocks in 6 to 8 absorbent dish towels or cloth napkins (it will feel like a well-bundled baby!). Place in the fridge and apply a bit of pressure to the blocks with a plate or other weight—it is okay if the tofu breaks into sections. Refrigerate for at least 24 hours to create a thicker consistency. You will notice the cloth become soaked with water from the tofu; replace with fresh outer dish towels as needed.

2. In a food processor, place the tofu, maple syrup, lime zest, and lime juice. Blend until smooth and there are no visible small flecks of tofu. Serve immediately or store in the fridge in an airtight container until ready to be gobbled up.

NOTE:

The tofu *must* be silken *and* firm or extra firm to work in this recipe. It's fine if it is also "lite."

VARIATION: LEMON FROSTING OR PUDDING

Use lemon zest and lemon juice instead of the lime zest and lime juice.

VARIATION: BERRY FROSTING OR PUDDING

Use lemon zest and lemon juice instead of lime zest and lime juice. Add 2 cups fresh or frozen raspberries, strawberries, blueberries, or blackberries.

OUR GERMAN CHOCOLATE FROSTING

MAKES ABOUT 1½ CUPS

1½ cups walnuts

½ cup maple syrup

1 tablespoon flaxseed meal

¼ teaspoon cinnamon

½ teaspoon vanilla

Need we say more? "Yum" says it all. At first blush, this frosting, traditionally used to top German Chocolate Cake, doesn't look like much, but once you taste it, your head will spin—directing you back for more!

In a food processor or high-speed blender, place the walnuts and 3 tablespoons water. Gently pulse until the walnuts break into smaller pieces—be careful not to grind them too much or they will turn into butter. Scrape down the sides of the processor if needed. Add the maple syrup, flaxseed meal, cinnamon, and vanilla. Process or pulse until the ingredients are mixed but some visible, small pieces of walnut remain—just like a classic German chocolate frosting texture.

SMOOTH SOFT SERVE

To make heart disease–friendly: Leave out the nuts and chocolate chips

SERVES 6

3 frozen ripe bananas, skin removed before freezing (see note)

OPTIONAL ADD-INS

Frozen cherries

Frozen mango chunks

Any frozen berries

OPTIONAL TOPPINGS

Chocolate balsamic vinegar (see page 95)

Toasted walnuts

Cinnamon

Nutmeg

Nondairy chocolate chips

This is our answer to soft-serve ice cream. It is truly stunning how similar it is. We use a Yonanas machine, an easy-to-use machine that truly creates fluffy, creamy soft serve! Each and every time we serve it people ask what else is in it. No one believes our response, "It is just frozen bananas!" The riper the bananas, the sweeter the "soft serve."

Place the bananas in the Yonanas machine (or whichever ice-cream maker you are using) with any add-ins you'd like (if using) and be amazed at what you have created. Sprinkle with your choice of toppings (if using).

NOTE:

If you are using a Yonanas machine, the frozen bananas may be used whole. Other machines may require the bananas to be sliced into sections before freezing—use your machine as directed.

ACKNOWLEDGMENTS

We are grateful beyond belief to the Plant-Based Women Warriors we may never meet—onward with plants, love, and each other!

A huge thank-you to Avery, an imprint of Penguin Random House, and InkWell for embracing Plant-Based Women Warriors. Megan, Lucia, and Richard, you make our publishing world go round! We fell hard for our copyeditor, Heather Rodino, when she mentioned eating our Lemon Oatmeal recipe during the copyediting process. And we are convinced our magical associate art director, Ashley Tucker, got her degree from Hogwarts! As ever, we remain in awe of Lucia's brilliant, warrior-style editing; it must come from all the plants she eats!

We owe more than anyone will ever know to our photographer, Karin McKenna, who arrived in our world packed with perfect photographer ingredients: flexibility, strength, backgrounds and props akimbo, and pure gameness! Karin has changed how we see food—it is all about the texture, flowers, and pot handles. Koyen and her chole remain a highlight of the photoshoot. And the lucky days Crile worked with us landed some of our most creative shots. The lovely women's table shoot was made complete with Susie Taft, Vanessa Hildebrand, and Karen Johnson.

Massive thanks to those who contributed recipes or recipe inspiration: Char Nolan, Travis Gay, Siri Benjamin, Beth Summers, Koyen Shah, Anne Bingham, Polly LaBarre, Brian Hart, Crile Hart, Bainon Hart, Zeb Hart, Flinn Esselstyn, Rose Esselstyn, Rip Esselstyn, Elizabeth Thornton, Jillian Gibson, Jackie Acho, Cindy Pierce, Kristin Brown, Pennie Rand, Elizabeth Keene, Mark LaMonda, Ben Czech, Brenda Reed, Peter McCoy, Susie Taft, Brooks Jones, Jim MacNamara, Audrey Kellermeyer, the Happy Pear—Stephen and David Flynn, and the brilliance of Nidhi Guria at PlantBasedIndianLiving.com.

Recipe testing is a task that sounds dreamy from the start, but it is a bear. Thanks to Tiff Cunningham, Cindy Pierce, Lisa Fedorovich, Theresa Cary, Darlene Kelbach, Sandie Sanjer, John

Fitzgerald, Eleanor Rimmerman, Maria Rimmerman, and Brenda Peterson for such heavy lifting. Also, testing thanks to Elizabeth Winings, Laurie Kortowich, Patrick Galvin, and Rob Hawkins.

Halley Moore, thank you for picking through rough, redundant first drafts.

Thank you to our whole, huge plant-based family: Essy, Ann, Rip, Ted, Jane, Zeb, Anne, Brian, Jill, Polly, Flinn, Gus, Rose, Crile, Zeb, Bainon, Georgie, Kole, Sophie, and Hope. May we all live with vitality, love, and connection.

Ann, Mommy, you've given so much to so many as the original fierce, bold Plant-Based Woman Warrior. What you have given me is best of all—so much togetherness.

This is Ann shouting out, "Thank you, Jane, because this book is YOU: the initial idea, the chapter ideas, most of the recipes, and most importantly, writing it all up because it would have been a total scramble coming from my computer!"

INDEX

Note: Page numbers in *italics* indicate photos. Recipe titles with asterisks (*) indicate heart disease–friendly recipes or recipe options.

A

African Peanut Soup, 139
Amaretto Cherry Chocolate Hazelnut Scones, *290*, 291
Amaretto Cookies, *276*, 277
Ann and Essy's Favorite Dressing*, *94*, 96
Ann's Arugula Salads (with citrus, beets, orange/dill, grapefruit/strawberry), *158*, 159–63
Ann's Open-Faced Twice-Baked Potatoes*, *262*, 263
Ann's Short Flax Biscuits*, *206*, 208
Ann's story, 11–13, 14–17
Ann's Warrior Oats*, *58*, 59
appetizers, sides, and extras, 177–99. *See also* brussels sprouts
    Barbecue Pulled Portobello Sliders with Green Goddess Sauce*, *184*, 185
    Butternut Squash Hunks*, 186
    Cauliflower Fritters*, *180*, 181
    Green Beans with Sesame Crumble*, *178*, 179
    Jillian's Quick Pickles*, *192*, 193
    Lucky Nuts, *196*, 197
    Roasted Cauliflower and Broccoli Bites*, *182*, 183
    Seed and Nut Bark, *198*, 199
    Smoky Barbecue Zucchini Rounds*, 186
    Top Ten Toppings for Air-Popped Popcorn, 187
apples
    Apple Flax Flapjacks*, *66*, 67
    Apple Sage Pan-Fried Tempeh*, 173
    Apple-Lidded Sandwich*, *114*, 115
    Bai's "No Rules" Sandwiches*, *122*, 123
    Wonder Woman Salad*, *148*, 149
avocados
    Avocado Pesto, 88

BLT&A and/or O Sandwich*, *112*, 113
bowls with, 219, 221, 233
Brooks's Bagel*, *116*, 117
#1 Guacamole, *102*, 107
Taco Bar*, *236*, 237

B

Bai's "No Rules" Sandwiches*, *122*, 123
Balanced Rice Noodle Bowl*, *226*, 227
Balsamic Hummus*, 91
bananas
    Breakfast Banana Muffins or Bread*, *62*, 63
    Smooth Soft Serve*, 309
Barbecue Pulled Portobello Sliders with Green Goddess Sauce*, *184*, 185
Baritone Dressing*, *94*, 97
barley bowl, *230*, 231
Basic Baked Tofu Cubes*, 167
Basic Pan-Fried Tempeh Cubes*, 167
beans and lentils. *See also* Hummus We Love*
    Bean Burgers in a Flash*, *240*, 241
    Big Bean Barley and Sweet Potato Soup*, *142*, 143
    bowls with, 219, 221, 227, 229, 231, 233
    Brian's Red Bean Chili*, *250*, 251
    Carrot Mushroom Red Lentil Soup*, *140*, 141
    Cheezy Chickpeas, 254
    Chickpea Masala (Chole), *244*, 245
    Crispy Checkin' Nuggets*, *242*, 243
    Curried Cauliflower Salad with Lentils and Grapes*, *154*, 155
    Falafel Wraps, Pockets, and Spears*, *128*, 129
    Gingered Chickpeas and Roasted Cherry Tomatoes over Black Rice*, *268*, 269

Jim's Kung Pao Chickpeas over Brown Rice*, *252*, 253
Loaded Vegetable Soup with Farro and Beans*, *136*, 137
New Senate Soup*, *134*, 135
Orange Mango Bean Salad*, *156*
Rainbow Bean Slaw*, *150*, 151
Taco Bar*, *236*, 237
Tune-In Salad*, *110*, 111
Woman Warrior Burgers*, 238–39, *240*
beet, dressing with, 100
beet salad, 160
berries
    Ann's Arugula Grapefruit Strawberry Salad*, *162*, 163
    Berry Frosting or Pudding, *306*, 307
    Blueberry Summer Corn Muffins*, *60*, 61
    Strawberry Balsamic Dressing*, *94*, 99
    Zander Tart, *286*, 287
Big Bean Barley and Sweet Potato Soup*, *142*, 143
Black Ramen Bowl*, *246*, 247
BLT&A and/or O Sandwich*, *112*, 113
blueberries. *See* berries
bowls, 215–35. *See also* salads
    about: building, 216, 217; overview of, 215–16
    Balanced Rice Noodle Bowl*, *226*, 227
    Black Ramen Bowl*, *246*, 247
    Braw Barley Bowl*, *230*, 231
    Buddha Bowl*, *220*, 221
    Flinn's Hummus Bowl*, *224*, 225
    Forbidden Bowl*, *218*, 219
    Groove-On Quinoa Bowl*, *232*, 233
    Pasta Tonight Bowl*, *234*, 235
    Roots and Shoots Bowl*, *222*, 223
    San Fran Savory Bowl*, *248*, 249
    Wide-Open Burrito Bowl*, *228*, 229
Boyfriend Bolognese Sauce*, 85

Braw Barley Bowl*, *230*, 231
breads and crackers, 201–13
  Ann's Short Flax Biscuits*, *206*, 208
  Blueberry Summer Corn Muffins*, *60*, 61
  Breakfast Banana Muffins or Bread*, *62*, 63
  Clava Cairn Soda Bread*, *212*, 213
  Jane's Tall Flax Biscuits, *206*, 207
  Naan Bread*, 209–11, *210*
  Quick and Easy Beer Bread*, *204*, 205
  Seed and Millet Crackers*, *202*, 203
breakfasts, 53–73. *See also* oats
  about: overview of, 53
  Apple Flax Flapjacks*, *66*, 67
  Blueberry Summer Corn Muffins*, *60*, 61
  Breakfast Banana Muffins or Bread*, *62*, 63
  Grits and Greens*, *70*, 71
  Open-Faced Chickpea Omelet 3.0*, 73
  Sweet Potato Start*, 72
Brian's Fresh Salsa*, *102*, 104
Brian's Red Bean Chili*, *250*, 251
Bright Quinoa Lime Mint Salad*, 153
broccoli
  bowls with, 225, 227, 235, 249
  Roasted Cauliflower and Broccoli Bites*, *182*, 183
Brooks's Bagel*, *116*, 117
brownies, *296*, 297, *298*, 299
brussels sprouts, *188*, 189–91
  about, 189
  Brussels Sprout Tots*, *188*, 191
  Buffalo Brussels*, *188*, 189
  Persephone Holiday Salad*, 152
  Sweet and Savory Brussels Sprouts*, *188*, 190
Buddha Bowl*, *220*, 221
Buffalo Brussels*, *188*, 189
burrito bowl, *228*, 229
Butternut Squash Hunks*, 186

C

cabbage
  bowls with, 219, 225, 231
  Flinn's Pickled Cabbage*, 194
  Rainbow Bean Slaw*, *150*, 151

sandwiches with, 121, 125, 127, 185
  Three Goddesses Salad*, *146*, 147
cancer, plants and, 16, 28, 29, 32, 41
Cardamom Lemon Courgette Cake*, *292*, 293
Carrot Mushroom Red Lentil Soup*, *140*, 141
cauliflower
  bowls with, 225, 235
  Cauliflower Fritters*, *180*, 181
  Curried Cauliflower Salad with Lentils and Grapes*, *154*, 155
Cheezy Chickpeas, 254
cherries, scones with, *290*, 291
Cherry Chunk Walnut Brownies, 297
chickpeas. *See* beans and lentils
chocolate
  Amaretto Cherry Chocolate Hazelnut Scones, *290*, 291
  Chocolate Gelato or Ganache, *304*, 305
  Creamy Chocolate Frosting or Pudding (and variation), *302*, 303
  Frosted Fudgy Walnut Brownies, *298*
  Mint Chip Brownies, 297
  Mint Chocolate Chip Frosting or Pudding, *302*, 303
  Our Chocolate Cake* with frosting variations, *300*, 301–2
  Our German Chocolate Frosting, 308
  Outta Sight Brownies, *296*, 297
cholesterol, 25
Chorizo Tempeh or Tofu*, 172
Cilantro-Mint Sauce, 83
citrus
  Ann's Arugula and Bright Orange Salad with Dill*, *158*, 161
  Ann's Arugula and Gorgeous Citrus Salad*, *158*, 159
  Ann's Arugula Grapefruit Strawberry Salad*, *162*, 163
  Cardamom Lemon Courgette Cake*, *292*, 293
  Crile's Light Lemon Dressing*, *94*, 98
  Gingered Minty Melon Balls in Orange Juice*, *284*, 285

Lemon Frosting or Pudding, *306*, 307
Lemon Hummus*, 91
Lemon Oatmeal*, *64*, 65
Lemon Pie Squares, *288*, 289
Lemon Tahini Sauce, 82
Lime Frosting or Pudding, *306*, 307
Lime Loves Watermelon and Watermelon Loves Lime*, *280*, 281
Orange Mango Bean Salad*, *156*
Orange-Lemon Cupcakes with Lime Frosting*, *294*, 295
Tangy Lime and Sweet Corn Sauce*, 79
Clava Cairn Soda Bread*, *212*, 213
collard wraps*, *124*, 125. *See also* greens
condiments, 47
Cool Cucumber Soup*, *130*, 131
corn
  Blueberry Summer Corn Muffins*, *60*, 61
  Corn Gazpacho*, *132*, 133
  Summer Corn Slab Open-Faced Sandwich*, *126*, 127
  Tangy Lime and Sweet Corn Sauce*, 79
  Top Ten Toppings for Air-Popped Popcorn, 187
Creamy Stuffed Sweet Potatoes*, *266*, 267
Crile's Light Lemon Dressing*, *94*, 98
Crispy Checkin' Nuggets*, *242*, 243
Crispy Vanilla Wafers*, *276*, 278
cucumbers
  Apple-Lidded Sandwich*, *114*, 115
  Cool Cucumber Soup*, *130*, 131
  Jillian's Quick Pickles*, *192*, 193
  Summer Garden Open-Faced Sandwich*, 121
Curried Cauliflower Salad with Lentils and Grapes*, *154*, 155
Cut-Out Oatmeal Cookies and Granola Bits, *276*, 279

D

desserts, 273–309. *See also* chocolate; frostings; tofu, desserts with
  about: overview of, 42

Amaretto Cherry Chocolate Hazelnut Scones, *290*, 291
Amaretto Cookies, *276*, 277
Cardamom Lemon Courgette Cake*, *292*, 293
Crispy Vanilla Wafers*, *276*, 278
Cut-Out Oatmeal Cookies and Granola Bits, *276*, 279
Gingered Minty Melon Balls in Orange Juice*, *284*, 285
Lemon Pie Squares, *288*, 289
Lime Loves Watermelon and Watermelon Loves Lime*, *280*, 281
Orange-Lemon Cupcakes with Lime Frosting*, *294*, 295
Pepparkakor* (Crispy Swedish Ginger Cookie), *274*, 275
Smooth Soft Serve*, 309
diabetes, plants and, 24–27
dinner recipes. *See also* bowls; sandwiches and wraps
    Ann's Open-Faced Twice-Baked Potatoes*, *262*, 263
    Brian's Red Bean Chili*, *250*, 251
    Cheezy Chickpeas, 254
    Chickpea Masala (Chole), *244*, 245
    Creamy Stuffed Sweet Potatoes*, *266*, 267
    Crispy Checkin' Nuggets*, *242*, 243
    Gingered Chickpeas and Roasted Cherry Tomatoes over Black Rice*, *268*, 269
    Jim's Kung Pao Chickpeas over Brown Rice*, *252*, 253
    Peter's Glazed Eggplant Cutlet with Brown Rice*, *264*, 265
    Plant-Based Pad Thai*, *255*–57, *256*
    Shepherdess Pie Topped with Tatties and Neeps*, *270*–71
    Sweet Potato and Cashew Ricotta Lasagna, *258*, 259–61, *260*

E

eggplant cutlet, *264*, 265

F

Falafel Wraps, Pockets, and Spears*, *128*, 129
farro, soup with, *136*, 137
flapjacks, *66*, 67

Flinn's Hummus Bowl*, *224*, 225
Flinn's Pickled Cabbage*, 194
flour (oat), making, 46
Forbidden Bowl*, *218*, 219
fridge staples, 46
frostings
    about: variations summaries, *302*, *306*
    Berry Frosting or Pudding, *306*, 307
    Creamy Chocolate Frosting or Pudding, *302*, 303
    Lemon Frosting or Pudding, *306*, 307
    Lime Frosting or Pudding, *306*, 307
    Mint Chocolate Chip Frosting or Pudding, *302*, 303
    Our German Chocolate Frosting, 308

G

garlic
    about: cooking onions, mushrooms and, 51; seasoning tip, 203
    Roasted Garlic Hummus*, 91, 92
gazpacho, corn, *132*, 133
ginger
    Gingered Chickpeas and Roasted Cherry Tomatoes over Black Rice*, *268*, 269
    Gingered Minty Melon Balls in Orange Juice*, *284*, 285
    Pepparkakor* (Crispy Swedish Ginger Cookie), *274*, 275
    Sesame Ginger Sauce*, 80
    Walnut Ginger Sauce and Dressing, 76
grapes
    Curried Cauliflower Salad with Lentils and Grapes*, *154*, 155
    Red Radish Grape Salsa*, *102*, 106
Green Beans with Sesame Crumble*, *178*, 179. *See also* Jillian's Quick Pickles*
Green Goddess Sauce and Dressing*, 81
greens. *See also* bowls; kale; salads
    Ann's Warrior Oats*, *58*, 59
    Grits and Greens*, *70*, 71
    Rose's Collard Wraps*, *124*, 125

sandwiches with, *116*, 119–20, 121, 123, 241
Groove-On Quinoa Bowl*, *232*, 233
guacamole, *102*, 107

H

heart health
    cholesterol and, 25
    Patricia's story, 26–27
    plants and, 12, 16–17, 26–27, 42–43
    recipes supporting, 42–43 (*See also recipe titles ending with asterisks (*)*)
herbs and spices, 47
Hickory Smokehouse Hummus*, 91, 92
hormonal/sexual health, 28–32
horseradish, in Walnut Horseradish Dressing, *94*, 99
Hummus We Love*, *90*, 91–93. *See also* Flinn's Hummus Bowl*
    Balsamic Hummus*, 91
    Black Bean Hummus*, 91
    Hickory Smokehouse Hummus*, 91, 92
    Lemon Hummus*, 91
    Roasted Garlic Hummus*, 91, 92
    sandwiches with, 115, 119–20, 121, 123, 125, *126*
    Thousand Island Hummus*, 93

I

immunity, 32–37
In the Pink Dressing*, *94*, 100

J

Jane's Ris-*Oat*-To Warrior Oats*, 59
Jane's Tall Flax Biscuits, *206*, 207
Jillian's Quick Pickles*, *192*, 193
Jim's Kung Pao Chickpeas over Brown Rice*, *252*, 253

K

kale
    about: cooking, 49
    bowls with, 221, 249
    breakfast oats with, 57, *58*, 59
    Grits and Greens*, *70*, 71
    salads with, 147, 149, 152
    sandwiches with, 121, 123, 125, 127, 241
    soup and chili with, 135, 251

L

lemon and lime. *See* citrus
Lightning Dressing*, *94*, 101
Loaded Vegetable Soup with
    Farro and Beans*, *136*, 137
Low-Fat Peanut Sauce*, 77
Lucky Nuts, *196*, 197

M

mangoes
    bowls with, 219, 223, 229, 233
    Orange Mango Bean Salad*,
      156
    Vibrant Mango Salsa*, *102*, 105
marinara sauce*, original, 84
melons
    Gingered Minty Melon Balls in
      Orange Juice*, *284*, 285
    Lime Loves Watermelon and
      Watermelon Loves Lime*,
      280, 281
    Watermelon Salsa*, *102*, 106
mint
    Bright Quinoa Lime Mint
      Salad*, 153
    Cilantro-Mint Sauce, 83
    Gingered Minty Melon Balls in
      Orange Juice*, *284*, 285
    Mint Chip Brownies, 297
    Mint Chocolate Chip Frosting or
      Pudding, *302*, 303
Mommy's Mushroom Gravy 3.0*,
    86, 87
Morning Commute Oats*, 56
multiple sclerosis, 34–35
mushrooms
    about: cooking onions, garlic
      and, 51
    Barbecue Pulled Portobello
      Sliders with Green Goddess
      Sauce*, *184*, 185
    Carrot Mushroom Red Lentil
      Soup*, *140*, 141
    Mommy's Mushroom Gravy
      3.0*, *86*, 87

N

Naan Bread*, 209–11, *210*
New Senate Soup*, *134*, 135
#1 Guacamole, *102*, 107
nuts and seeds
    African Peanut Soup, 139
    Amaretto Cherry Chocolate
      Hazelnut Scones, *290*, 291
    Amaretto Cookies, *276*, 277

Ann's Short Flax Biscuits*, *206*,
    208
Apple Flax Flapjacks*, *66*, 67
Cashew Pesto, 89
Cherry Chunk Walnut
    Brownies, 297
Flax Biscuits, *206*, 207–8
Frosted Fudgy Walnut
    Brownies, *298*
Green Goddess Sauce and
    Dressing*, 81
Lemon Tahini Sauce, 82
Low-Fat Peanut Sauce*, 77
Lucky Nuts, *196*, 197
other desserts with, 279, 287,
    289, 297, 308
Pan-Toasted Pepita Granola*,
    54, 55
Peanut Butter Gelato or
    Ganache, *304*, 305
salads with, 147, 149, 152, 159,
    160
Seed and Millet Crackers*, *202*,
    203
Seed and Nut Bark, *198*, 199
Sesame Ginger Sauce*, 80
Siri's Breakfast Pucks, *68*, 69
Spicy Almond Sauce, 78
Sweet Potato and Cashew
    Ricotta Lasagna, *258*, 259–61,
    260
Thai Peanut Sauce, 77
Walnut Ginger Sauce and
    Dressing, 76
Walnut Horseradish Dressing,
    94, 99
Walnut Pesto, 88

O

oats
    about: making flour, 46
    Ann's Warrior Oats*, *58*, 59
    Cut-Out Oatmeal Cookies and
      Granola Bits, *276*, 279
    Jane's Ris-*Oat*-To Warrior Oats*,
      59
    Lemon Oatmeal*, *64*, 65
    Morning Commute Oats*, 56
    Om Oats*, 57
    Pan-Toasted Pepita Granola*,
      54, 55
    Polly's Powered-Up Warrior
      Oats*, 59
    Seed and Millet Crackers*, *202*,
      203

Siri's Breakfast Pucks, *68*, 69
Om Oats*, 57
onions
    about: caramelizing, 50;
      cooking garlic, mushrooms
      and, 51; seasoning tip, 203
    BLT&A and/or O Sandwich*,
      112, 113
    Brooks's Bagel*, *116*, 117
    Pickled Purple Onion with
      Parsley*, 195
oranges. *See* citrus
Original Marinara*, 84
Our Chocolate Cake* with frosting
    variations, *300*, 301–2
Our German Chocolate Frosting,
    308
Outta Sight Brownies, *296*, 297

P

pad Thai*, 255–57, *256*
pancakes, *66*, 67
Pan-Toasted Pepita Granola*, *54*,
    55
pantry staples, 46, 47
parsnips, 138, *222*, 233
pasta
    Black Ramen Bowl*, *246*, 247
    other bowls with noodles, 219,
      227
    Pasta Tonight Bowl*, *234*, 235
    Plant-Based Pad Thai*, 255–57,
      256
    Sweet Potato and Cashew
      Ricotta Lasagna, *258*, 259–61,
      260
Patricia's story, 26–27
Peach Melba*, *282*, 283
Peach Salsa*, *102*, 103
peanuts. *See* nuts and seeds
Pepparkakor* (Crispy Swedish
    Ginger Cookie), 274, 275
Persephone Holiday Salad*, 152
pestos, 88–89
Peter's Glazed Eggplant Cutlet
    with Brown Rice*, *264*, 265
pickles
    Flinn's Pickled Cabbage*, 194
    Jillian's Quick Pickles*, *192*, 193
    Pickled Purple Onion with
      Parsley*, 195
plant-based eating. *See also* Plant-
    Based Women Warriors
    finding food freedom and,
      22–23

flavor importance, 40

general guidelines and book overview, 42–43

hormonal/sexual health and, 28–32

immunity and, 32–37

kitchen staples and cooking basics, 45–51

lifestyle disease protection, 24–28 (*See also* cancer; diabetes; heart health)

Plant-Based Pad Thai*, 255–57, *256*

Plant-Based Women Warriors

Ann's story, energy and "hop-to" at eighty-six, 11–13, 14–17

becoming, 14–17

Char's story, 41

grandchildren on being plant-based, 13–14

Jordi's story, 30–31

Joyce's story, 33

Lily's story, 28

live long, die fast challenge, 12

Monica's story, 36–37

Patricia's story, 26–27

Saray's story, 34–35

Polly's Powered-Up Warrior Oats*, 59

popcorn toppings, 187

potatoes

about: cooking, 49

Ann's Open-Faced Twice-Baked Potatoes*, *262*, 263

bowls with, 223, 247, 249

New Senate Soup*, *134*, 135

Shepherdess Pie Topped with Tatties and Neeps*, 270–71

Q

Quick and Easy Beer Bread*, *204*, 205

quinoa

Bright Quinoa Lime Mint Salad*, 153

Groove-On Quinoa Bowl*, *232*, 233

Taco Bar*, *236*, 237

Woman Warrior Burgers*, 238–39, *240*

R

radish grape salsa*, red, *102*, 106

radishes, in Apple-Lidded Sandwich*, *114*, 115

Rainbow Bean Slaw*, *150*, 151

rice and rice noodles

bowls with, 219, 221, 225, 227, 229, 247, 249

Gingered Chickpeas and Roasted Cherry Tomatoes over Black Rice*, *268*, 269

Jim's Kung Pao Chickpeas over Brown Rice*, *252*, 253

Peter's Glazed Eggplant Cutlet with Brown Rice*, *264*, 265

Taco Bar*, *236*, 237

Roasted Cauliflower and Broccoli Bites*, *182*, 183

Roasted Garlic Hummus*, 91, 92

Rock-Around-the-Clock Grilled Wrap*, *118*, 119–20

Romaine Dippers, 92

Roots and Shoots Bowl*, *222*, 223

Rose's Collard Wraps*, *124*, 125

S

salads, 145–63. *See also* bowls

Ann's Arugula Salads (with citrus, beets, orange/dill, grapefruit/strawberry), *158*, 159–63

Bright Quinoa Lime Mint Salad*, 153

Curried Cauliflower Salad with Lentils and Grapes*, *154*, 155

Orange Mango Bean Salad*, *156*

Persephone Holiday Salad*, 152

Rainbow Bean Slaw*, *150*, 151

Romaine Dippers, 92

Three Goddesses Salad*, *146*, 147

Tune-In Salad*, *110*, 111

Wonder Woman Salad*, *148*, 149

salsa and guacamole, 102, 103–7

Brian's Fresh Salsa*, *102*, 104

#1 Guacamole, *102*, 107

Peach Salsa*, *102*, 103

Red Radish Grape Salsa*, *102*, 106

Vibrant Mango Salsa*, *102*, 105

Watermelon Salsa*, *102*, 106

San Fran Savory Bowl*, *248*, 249

sandwiches and wraps

Apple-Lidded Sandwich*, *114*, 115

Bai's "No Rules" Sandwiches*, *122*, 123

Barbecue Pulled Portobello Sliders with Green Goddess Sauce*, *184*, 185

Bean Burgers in a Flash*, *240*, 241

BLT&A and/or O Sandwich*, *112*, 113

Brooks's Bagel*, *116*, 117

Crispy Checkin' Nuggets* with, *242*, 243

Falafel Wraps, Pockets, and Spears*, *128*, 129

Rock-Around-the-Clock Grilled Wrap*, *118*, 119–20

Rose's Collard Wraps*, *124*, 125

Summer Corn Slab Open-Faced Sandwich*, *126*, 127

Summer Garden Open-Faced Sandwich*, 121

Taco Bar*, *236*, 237

Woman Warrior Burgers*, 238–39, *240*

sauces and dressings. *See also* Hummus We Love*; salsa and guacamole

about: vinegars, 47, 95

Ann and Essy's Favorite Dressing*, *94*, 96

Avocado Pesto, 88

Baritone Dressing*, *94*, 97

Boyfriend Bolognese Sauce*, 85

Cashew Pesto, 89

Cilantro-Mint Sauce, 83

Crile's Light Lemon Dressing*, *94*, 98

Green Goddess Sauce and Dressing*, 81

Lemon Tahini Sauce, 82

Lightning Dressing*, *94*, 101

Low-Fat Peanut Sauce*, 77

Mommy's Mushroom Gravy 3.0*, *86*, 87

Original Marinara*, 84

In the Pink Dressing*, *94*, 100

Sesame Ginger Sauce*, 80

Spicy Almond Sauce, 78

Strawberry Balsamic Dressing*, *94*, 99

Tangy Lime and Sweet Corn Sauce*, 79

Teriyaki Sauce*, 76

Thai Peanut Sauce, 77

3-2-1 Hum Dressing*, *94*, 97

Walnut Ginger Sauce and Dressing, 76

Walnut Horseradish Dressing, *94*, 99

sauces and dressings (continued)
  Walnut Pesto, 88
Savory Tofu or Tempeh Cubes*, 174, 175
seeds. See nuts and seeds
Sesame Ginger Sauce*, 80
Sesame Ginger–Topped Tofu or Tempeh, 170, 171
sexual/hormonal health, 28–32
Shepherdess Pie Topped with Tatties and Neeps*, 270–71
Siri's Breakfast Pucks, 68, 69
Smoky Barbecue Zucchini Rounds*, 186
Smooth Soft Serve*, 309
soda bread, 212, 213
soft serve, 309
soups
  African Peanut Soup, 139
  Big Bean Barley and Sweet Potato Soup*, 142, 143
  Brian's Red Bean Chili*, 250, 251
  Carrot Mushroom Red Lentil Soup*, 140, 141
  Cool Cucumber Soup*, 130, 131
  Corn Gazpacho*, 132, 133
  Loaded Vegetable Soup with Farro and Beans*, 136, 137
  New Senate Soup*, 134, 135
  New Year's Parsnip Soup*, 138
spices and herbs, 47
Spicy Almond Sauce, 78
squash appetizers, 186
strawberries. See berries
Summer Corn Slab Open-Faced Sandwich*, 126, 127
Summer Garden Open-Faced Sandwich*, 121
Sweet and Savory Brussels Sprouts*, 188, 190
sweet potatoes
  about: brownies with, 299; cooking, 48
  Bai's "No Rules" Sandwiches*, 122, 123
  Big Bean Barley and Sweet Potato Soup*, 142, 143

bowls with, 219, 221, 223, 249
Creamy Stuffed Sweet Potatoes*, 266, 267
Sweet Potato and Cashew Ricotta Lasagna, 258, 259–61, 260
Sweet Potato Start*, 72
Taco Bar*, 236, 237
Woman Warrior Burgers*, 238–39, 240

T

Taco Bar*, 236, 237
Tangy Lime and Sweet Corn Sauce*, 79
tempeh. See tofu and tempeh
Teriyaki Sauce*, 76
Teriyaki Tofu or Tempeh Cubes*, 168, 169
Thai Peanut Sauce, 77
Thousand Island Hummus*, 93
Three Goddesses Salad*, 146, 147
3-2-1 Hum Dressing*, 94, 97
tofu, desserts with
  about: buying tofu for, 166
  Creamy Chocolate Frosting or Pudding (and variation), 302, 303
  Lime Frosting or Pudding (and Lemon or Berry variations), 306, 307
  Peach Melba*, 282, 283
  Peanut Butter Gelato or Ganache (and variations), 304, 305
  Zander Tart, 286, 287
tofu and tempeh, 165–75
  about: overview of recipes, 165; pressing, prepping tofu, 166; tofu to buy, 165–66
  Apple Sage Pan-Fried Tempeh*, 173
  Bai's "No Rules" Sandwiches*, 122, 123
  Basic Baked Tofu Cubes*, 167
  Basic Pan-Fried Tempeh Cubes*, 167

BLT&A and/or O Sandwich*, 112, 113
bowls with, 219, 221, 223, 227, 229, 233, 247
Boyfriend Bolognese Sauce* (tempeh), 85
Chorizo Tempeh or Tofu*, 172
Plant-Based Pad Thai*, 255–57, 256
Savory Tofu or Tempeh Cubes*, 174, 175
Sesame Ginger–Topped Tofu or Tempeh, 170, 171
Taco Bar*, 236, 237
Teriyaki Tofu or Tempeh Cubes*, 168, 169
tomatoes. See also salsa and guacamole
  Boyfriend Bolognese Sauce*, 85
  Gingered Chickpeas and Roasted Cherry Tomatoes over Black Rice*, 268, 269
  Original Marinara*, 84
  sandwiches with (See sandwiches and wraps)
Tune-In Salad*, 110, 111
turnips, Shepherdess Pie with, 270–71

V

vanilla wafers*, 276, 278
vegetable soup, 136, 137
Vibrant Mango Salsa*, 102, 105
vinegars, 47, 95

W

walnuts. See nuts and seeds
watermelon. See melons
Wide-Open Burrito Bowl*, 228, 229
Woman Warrior Burgers*, 238–39, 240
Wonder Woman Salad*, 148, 149

Z

Zander Tart, 286, 287
zucchini rounds, 186